GYPSIES

UNDER THE

SWASTIKA

Also by Donald Kenrick

Gypsies: From the Ganges to the Thames
The Romani World: A historical dictionary of the Gypsies

GYPSIES

UNDER THE

SWASTIKA

Donald Kenrick and Grattan Puxon

University of Hertfordshire Press

First published in Great Britain in 2009 by
University of Hertfordshire Press
Learning and Information Services
University of Hertfordshire
College Lane
Hatfield
Hertfordshire AL10 9AB

British Library Cataloguing in Publication Data
A catalogue record for this book is available from the British Library

ISBN 978-1-902806-80-8

Design by DesignForBooks.co.uk
Cover design by John Robertshaw, Harpenden, AL5 2JB
Printed in Great Britain by Hobbs the Printers, Totton, SO40 3WX

CONTENTS

ILLUSTRATIONS

SONGS

GLOSSARY

Central Police Office Translation of *Reichskriminalpolizeiamt* or *RKPA*.

Central Security Headquarters Translation of *Reichsicherheitshauptamt* or *RSHA*.

German In the Second World War the German people as a whole were identified with the Nazis (National Socialists) by the victims. Generally, survivors' accounts will use the term 'German' rather than 'Nazi'.

Gypsy The term is used, when discussing policies, to translate terms such as *Zigeuner* in documents. It has been capitalised throughout.

Rom and **Sinto** (*pl.* Sinti) The two largest clans of Gypsies living in Europe, the Sinti mainly in Germany. The term 'Sinto' may originate from the province of Sindh.

Romani The language spoken by the Romanies.

Romany An ethnic group originating in north India. The term is used in the first historical chapter and later when ethnicity is important. Probably derived from a north Indian word *Dom*, meaning 'human being'.

PREFACE

The first edition of this book — entitled *The Destiny of Europe's Gypsies* — was published by Sussex University Press in 1972. It was originally intended to recount only the story of the Nazi persecution of the Gypsies — a story which, more than twenty-five years after Germany's defeat, had not yet been told. It soon became apparent to the authors that this episode in the history of the Romany people could not be regarded in isolation. It formed part of a chain of harassment and persecution based on prejudice deep-rooted in European society. Hence, the first chapter is entitled 'The roots of prejudice'. Accounts by survivors of the Nazi period are interwoven in the later chapters to highlight the effect of government policies and decrees on individual Roma and Sinti.

In 1995 a shortened version bearing the present title appeared in the Interface collection, sponsored by the Gypsy Research Centre in Paris. Now this new English-language edition has given me the opportunity to revise the text where further documentation has become available and to correct some typographical errors. However, the section on Romania is the only major change.

This remains the only book in any language which covers the fate of the Gypsies during this period throughout Europe, including at the hands of Germany's allies and puppet states. Nothing has been published since 1995 to change the authors' view that the ultimate aim of the Nazis was the elimination of all Gypsies.

Gypsies under the Swastika ends with the liberation of the camps and the end of the Second World War. Unfortunately, this has not meant the liberation of the Gypsy people from the subtler pressures of neglect and forced assimilation that just as surely threaten them with extinction as a separate people; nor, sad to say, an end to genocide in the world.

DONALD KENRICK
LONDON 2008

INTRODUCTION:

THE ROMANIES COME TO EUROPE

North India was the cradle of the Romany Gypsies and their language. There are no contemporary accounts of the first families from India to reach Persia on their long road westward to Europe, but the Persian poet Firdausi, writing in the tenth century, dates their arrival to some five centuries before his own time. He tells of 10,000 musicians sent from India to Shah Bahram Gur (who reigned AD 430–443) to entertain his people with their music.

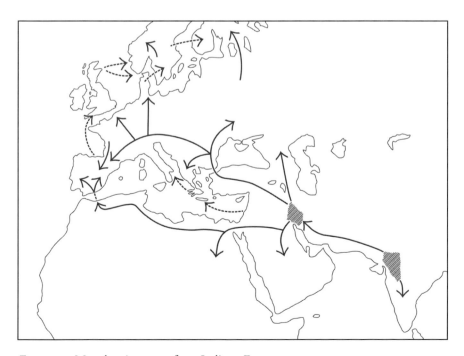

FIGURE I. Map showing route from India to Europe

Linguistic and other evidence shows that the Romanies of Europe belong to groups which left India between the fifth and eleventh centuries. Some crossed the Bosphorus into the Balkans, while others followed the route of returning pilgrims across the Mediterranean islands to southern Greece and Italy. Nomads are recorded 'stopping only 30 days in one place' in Crete as early as 1322 and settled shoemakers were already in the Balkans by 1483. Many Romanies had already moved west as the Turks advanced into Europe.

By the beginning of the sixteenth century there were several hundred Romanies in Europe, belonging to different clans and practising various trades. In the first chapter we look at their treatment as a small and vulnerable minority, a treatment which was to culminate in the horrors of the Nazi period.

THE ROOTS OF PREJUDICE

THE DARK STRANGERS

The Romanies' first appearance in Europe can be compared with that of modern-day migrants from Asia. They came in small family groups seeking opportunities to carry on their trades and occupations among existing settled populations. There was little space for them to establish their own homeland as earlier migrating peoples had done: every territory had already been staked out by other races. The only place left for them was therefore on the fringes of established society, where they had to make a living as best they could.

Smithing and metalworking of various forms were major occupations, although we can presume that other trades were also undertaken. Fortune-telling was hardly more than a sideline but, because of their palmistry and use of herbs, the Greeks called them by the name of a heretical sect, *atsin-gani*. From this are derived the words *Zigeuner*, *tsigane* and so on, as used in numerous languages. The English word 'Gypsy' and French *gitan*, on the other hand, are corruptions of 'Egyptian', the name by which the Romanies became known in several countries during the Middle Ages because of a belief among some groups that they had been expelled from Egypt.

Their true origins, however, were unknown, and when the Romanies crossed into Europe they appeared as if from nowhere — an unknown, alien people. They made a vivid impression on medieval society. Curious towns-folk of every class flocked to stare at them, to have their palms read or to watch acrobats and to buy hand-made goods. They were regarded at first as an amusing diversion. However, the conviction that blackness denotes inferiority and evil was already well-rooted in the European mind, and the nearly black skins of many Gypsies marked them out as victims of this prejudice. Even in Asia Firdausi had written 'no washing ever whitens the black Gypsy'. The monk Cornerius of Lübeck, reporting on Gypsies he had encountered in 1417, refers to their 'most ugly faces, black like those of Tartars'. Most absurd of the racialist arguments about blackness was the accusation by a Spanish judge that, despite the disadvantages of being black in a white society, Gypsies deliberately darkened themselves using vegetable dyes. In Finland, Archdeacon Cajanus, convinced of this practice, issued an order in 1663 that Gypsies must not be permitted to blacken their children in future. In 1619 Sancho de Moncada, Professor of Theology at the University of Toledo in Spain, condemned the speaking of a secret language as one of the Gypsies' sins. It was many years before Romani was recognised as a fully fledged language of Indian origin.

The Gypsies' apparent lack of roots or attachment to any known land was a reason for widespread speculation about their origin, with one medieval writer calling them 'a race of Jews who later became mixed with Christian vagabonds'. Attitudes to the Romanies right across Europe varied little; it is a European phenomenon we are dealing with in which the different social groups — peasants, clergy and rulers — have all played their part.

THE CHURCH AND THE GUILDS

Another strong factor in the unfavourable attitude towards Gypsies in western and central Europe was the suspicion attached to anyone who crossed from the Turkish-occupied lands. From that direction came infidels, enemies of the secular states and the Church. Lacking an organised religion of their own, the Gypsy people were from the beginning open to attack by Christian and indeed Muslim clergy. A widespread and sometimes fatal intolerance developed because Gypsies failed to practise with any conviction one or other of the prevalent religions. The Church in Europe generally rejected the Gypsy people even when they professed to be converts to Christianity. Their claim to be Christians expelled from Egypt by the Muslims carried little weight. In Holland the label *Heidens* — Heathens — adhered to them for centuries.

The clergy lent their weight wherever they exercised power. Thus Pope Pius V, as head of the Papal States, ordered male Gypsies to be sent to the galleys to serve at the battle of Lepanto and he expelled from Rome a humanitarian monk who dared to oppose this order. That some Protestant clergy shared the antagonism of the Catholics towards Gypsies is shown by the words of a Lithuanian minister in 1787: 'Gypsies in a well-ordered state are like vermin on an animal's body'.

Suspicion and dislike of newly arrived Gypsies by the three pillars of power in medieval Europe — the Church, the state and the trade guilds — soon hardened into entrenched opposition. Gypsies found themselves ever more frequently rejected. Curtailment of normal Gypsy occupations by the jealous craft guilds added to their difficulties. Gypsies not only carried out blacksmithing and repair work, but also made vessels and tools. Some clans produced baskets, combs and jewellery, selling them in the market at low prices. The guild masters would not tolerate this threat posed by wandering vagrants, as they saw them, to even a part of their monopoly. Barriers to normal business were sometimes formidable. The Guild of Locksmiths at Miskolc in Hungary canvassed successfully in 1740 for an order stopping Gypsies doing any metalwork outside their tents. As can be imagined, this restricted them to small operations.

The pressures on them unfortunately resulted in some Gypsies resorting to petty crime and trickery to get money for food. Their position on the fringes of society had been precarious at the best of times, but henceforth some of them, in western Europe in particular, were compelled to live on their wits, begging and poaching where they could. An unfavourable image of all Gypsies developed in the popular mind. Less than fifty years after the first Gypsy groups reached western Europe in 1407, the authorities began to receive a growing number of complaints.

GUILT

Distrust was further nurtured through the dissemination of stories purporting to illustrate not only the wrong-doings of Gypsies but the supposed guilt attached to being a Gypsy. It was said, for example, that Gypsies had been cursed by God because they had refused shelter in their tents to Joseph and Mary on their flight from Egypt.

Somewhere in the myths concerning earlier sins, impure blood and magic was born the least well-founded accusation of all: cannibalism. In Turkey and Albania it was thought that Gypsies commonly dug up graves and ate corpses. Part of the explanation may lie in the fact that Gypsies in these countries often buried their dead in unmarked graves and so local people may never have seen a Gypsy tomb. One of the most infamous trials for cannibalism occurred in Hungary in 1782. Almost 200 Gypsies were arrested and charged with this crime and systematically tortured until they confessed. As a result eighteen women were beheaded, fifteen men hanged, six men broken on the wheel and two quartered. A further 150 Gypsies were in prison still waiting their turn to die when the Emperor Joseph II sent a commission to investigate the case and discovered that the confessions were false. The persons who had allegedly been eaten were still alive.

Fortunately the Gypsies arrived too late in Europe to be blamed for spreading the Black Death, as were the Jews, yet over the centuries they have been continually accused of bringing dirt and disease. It is the most common myth about them and yet is the least often challenged. The fear of sickness from Gypsy encampments persists. Alleged to be bringing cholera to certain districts in Italy during 1910, for example, the Gypsies were driven away by local residents who armed themselves as vigilantes. Then a medical inspection showed the Gypsies had no trace of the disease.

Within Gypsy life, however, considerable importance is given to cleanliness. For the very reason that families are often forced to take up temporary residence on waste ground, where rubbish from householders tends to collect, rules on hygiene have to be strict. Numerous regulations were codified in a body of traditions and taboos, called by some groups the *Romania* and upheld by the *Kris* or council of elders. Were it not for this emphasis on hygiene and the authority of the elders in every camp to maintain standards, the Gypsies would hardly have survived.

EXPULSION

Leave or be hounded to death. This became the choice constantly forced upon Gypsies in most of Europe. Relegated to the position of an outcast minority, they faced banishment from one country after another. Such a stream of legislation flowed out from governments and parliaments that it is not practicable even to outline all the decrees. This historical ground has been well covered in other studies and we shall merely survey the various policies pursued.[1] Suffice to say that the historian Robert Scott Macfie listed 148 orders and decrees passed in the German states alone between 1416 and 1774.

England imposed the death penalty for being a Gypsy in 1554. In York nine people were executed under this law in 1596, while Elizabeth I added to the decree 'those who are or shall become of the fellowship or company of Egyptians'. The rising crescendo of legislation against Gypsies was linked in part with the consolidation of national states and a lowered tolerance towards minorities. When Emperor Maximilian I reaffirmed Germany's laws in 1500, Gypsies got notice to quit the land by Easter of the following year. The Emperor's legislators in this instance had accused the Gypsy community of being spies for a foreign power. The charge, first uttered during a debate in the Diet of the Empire in 1497, has persisted into modern times.

In 1709 the district of Ober-Rhein ordered any Gypsies taken by the authorities to be deported or sent to the galleys, even if no charges had been made against them. Five years later Mainz decreed the execution of all Gypsy men captured, and the flogging and branding of women and children.

However unjustified they might have been, the cumulative effect of the widespread anti-Gypsy laws was to make Gypsies non-citizens. No longer protected by the law, those who avoided arrest and expulsion by the official agents of order could be abused and mistreated and their belongings stolen with impunity by anyone. In one case the judge ruled that 'by taking the life of a Gypsy the defendant did not act against the policy of the state'.

To encourage active participation in driving out Gypsies, bounties were widely offered. Public posters in the German states offered a reward for anyone who brought in a Gypsy dead or alive.

SURVIVAL

Gypsies continued a precarious existence thanks only to the slow communications between central governments and local officials, the inaccessibility of certain regions and at times the shelter and patronage of well-placed aristocrats. They were compelled to follow a constant circuit from one country or district to another. The provinces they entered intensified measures against them while, in those they vacated, laws lapsed. Viewed in retrospect, killings could only have been selective whatever the letter of the law. The machinery for control and extermination did not exist until a later date.

Armed resistance became the last resort of a few desperate people. More common was retreat into remote areas. When central government, monopolising the enactment of new laws, could employ no speedier agent than a horseman, outlying districts sometimes offered relative shelter to fugitives. Thus, for example, the Basque region in France proved safe for many years until in 1802 the republican Prefect of the locality ordered the combing-out of Gypsies in his territory.

ASSIMILATION AND CONTAINMENT

From the fifteenth century to the present day, and often co-existing with more bloody measures, assimilation reveals itself as a long-drawn-out conspiracy to sever the roots of Gypsy life. Almost every European country has at one time or another outlawed nomadism, as nomads are viewed with suspicion. Spain curtailed the right as long ago as 1492. For the first scheme for mass assimilation we must move forward to the eighteenth century and the policies of Maria Theresa of Hungary. From 1761 onwards she issued a series of decrees intended to turn Gypsies into 'New Hungarians'. The Empress handed out seed and cattle to them and in return expected them to become good farmers. Under her plans, government-built huts replaced tents, and travel and horse-dealing were forbidden.

In general the authorities had to come to terms with the continued presence of Romanies and those that did not press at once for direct assimilation sought instead to contain the Romany population. Numerous special laws were enacted for this purpose. For example, in 1759 the Czarist government in Russia ruled it an offence for Gypsies to enter St Petersburg. In many parts of eastern Europe Gypsies have lived in separate quarters up to the present time.

THE NOBLE SAVAGE

The Romanies were often held in esteem by the nobility, an attitude which contrasted with the antipathy felt by the general population. They provided a lively diversion and neither competed with, nor threatened, the world of the aristocrats. Early on it became the habit of rich gentry to invite Romany entertainers, with their music and dancing, into their homes. Landowners protected them from the harsh laws. Many remained in refuge on nobles' estates. A special decree was issued in France in 1682 by which any aristocrat sheltering Gypsies would forfeit his lands to the crown.

And amid the anti-Gypsy writings one could find a nobler view of the people and their way of life. Thus, in Cervantes' story *La Gitanilla*, written in 1613, a Gypsy woman says:

We are the lords of the plain, of the crops, of the woods, of the forests, of the wells and of the streams. The forests supply us wood free of charge, the trees fruit, the vine grapes, the garden vegetables, the fountains water, the streams fish and the reserves game, the rock shade, the hills fresh air and the caves houses. We sleep as easily on the ground as in the softest bed. We are insensible to pain.

The Gypsies' bright clothing, carefree manner and lively musical abilities have all been portrayed frequently by writers and composers, one of the most famous being Bizet, whose opera *Carmen* was first produced in 1855. Indeed the nineteenth century saw an upsurge in romantic writing and feeling about the Romany people and went a long way towards transforming their popular image. From then onwards, alongside the stereotypical dirty, dishonest, child-stealing villain, we have the dark, handsome, violin-playing lover Gypsy, a 'noble savage' camping in the woodlands and living off the earth. Both are far from the truth and neither in the long run have done much to help the Romany people obtain recognition and minimum respect.

PRELUDE TO GENOCIDE

The picture that has been painted in this chapter is sadly a very negative one: attempts at expulsion followed by repression and forced assimilation. It is sometimes asked whether there was a golden age for Romanies in Europe, a time when they were not persecuted and were allowed to develop their culture and skills in freedom; the answer is probably yes. There were periods when Romanies had a recognised role — as horse dealers, smiths and musicians. In eastern and central Europe, in particular, they formed an integral part of society. However low their position, they occupied a place in their community. Some served as mercenary soldiers in different armies. The Romanies who found it easiest to escape from the general harassment were musicians, ranging from a harpist who played for Queen Victoria to the lady violinist Palaczinta in Romania, who was honoured with her portrait on a postage stamp.

Across Europe, however, the twentieth century brought the rise of a more bureaucratic society and demands for more control. In 1922 the German state of Baden introduced a certificate to be carried by nomads and five years later Prussia fingerprinted 8,000 Gypsies. Bavaria passed measures to prevent

Gypsies from travelling and camping in large family groups. They could not possess sporting guns and anyone over sixteen years of age without regular employment could be sent to a workhouse. For those not born in Bavaria deportation was decreed.

Everywhere the seeds of anti-Gypsy feeling fell on fertile ground and prepared the way for later events. The story up to this point can be seen as establishing the Gypsies as unloved outsiders — the prelude to the coming genocide.

CHAPTER

THE NON-ARYAN ARYANS

ALIENS IN EUROPE

When the Nazi (National Socialist) party came to power in Germany in 1933 they inherited anti-Gypsy laws already in operation. The attitude of the general public to the Romanies had long been one of mistrust and the new government certainly held no romantic feelings toward them. The new rulers quickly established a racial hierarchy with the 'Aryan' Germans at the top. Although Romani is a language in the Indo-Aryan group, the Nazis never recognised the Gypsies as Aryans. When two laws passed in 1935 made 'non-Europeans' second-class citizens, the standard legal commentaries considered the Gypsies to be in this category. Thus Stuckart and Globke: 'In Europe generally only Jews and Gypsies are of foreign blood.'[2]

Nazi journals, in particular *Volk und Rasse*, regularly printed articles on the Gypsy problem. The quotations cited below support the view that the Gypsies were considered as non-Aryans from the beginning of the Nazi period. Although later 'scientific' study of the Gypsies was concerned to demonstrate their anti-social nature, this was true, also, of the study of the Jews. They, too, had to be shown to be anti-social in their behaviour.

'A FOREIGN ELEMENT'

In this section the ideas expounded by Nazi writers are outlined, ideas upon which future policy was to be based. The articles show a considerable consensus of opinion on the subject of the Gypsies. All agree that they are of

11

Indian origin but have become mixed on their journey. As early as 1929, in his *Anthropology of Europe*, which has been called 'the Bible of Nazi anthropology', Professor Hans Gunther had already written:

> The Gypsies have indeed retained some elements from their Nordic home, but they are descended from the lowest classes of the population in that region. In the course of their migration they have absorbed the blood of the surrounding peoples and have thus become an Oriental, Western Asiatic racial mixture, with an addition of Indian, Mid-Asiatic and European strains . . . Their nomadic mode of living is a result of this mixture. The Gypsies will generally affect Europe as aliens.

This line of reasoning was followed by Dr R. Körber in 1936, in an article called 'Volk und Staat' ('Nation and State'): 'The Jew and the Gypsy are today far removed from us because their Asiatic ancestors were totally different from our Nordic forefathers'; an anonymous author in *SS Leitheft* wrote that 'the Gypsies originate from India and have taken into themselves the most varied mixture of other races during their journey through Persia, etc.'; while K. Rüdiger in *Volk und Rasse* said: 'The Gypsies are completely different in nature from us and obey other rules of life. They are a foreign element in every nation.'

Also in the journal *Volk und Rasse*, H. Schubert argued that 'only the Jews and Gypsies regularly count as foreign [*artfremd*] in Europe'. He divided the population of Europe into four groups: German and similar races; foreign races; Jewish and Gypsy; and coloured.

The writers claimed that the Gypsies were immoral, criminal, work-shy and ineducable. Statistics were cited to show Gypsies to be a burden on the social services. Thus *Volk und Rasse* pointed out in 1938 that some parishes in the Burgenland (Austria) had to pay large sums out for the maternity costs of Gypsy mothers. Gypsies represented a further danger because of their high birth rate, as Rüdiger noted: 'Their fertility is above that of the host nation. Ten to fourteen children is no rarity.'

We may note that in none of the above is any distinction made between sedentary and nomadic Gypsies. Dr G. Küppers, again in 1938, did admit in *Volk und Rasse*, however, that the nomads (as opposed to the sedentary Gypsies) often had 'friendly characteristics'. It was his opinion, nevertheless, that measures had to be taken against them also. The majority of writers treated

FIGURE 2. Front page of Nazi journal *NS Rechtspiegel*

the Gypsies, whether nomadic or sedentary, as a homogeneous group, except that it was suggested by some that part-Gypsies were worse than pure Gypsies, a suggestion that was to affect future legislation.

THE SOLUTIONS

We now turn to the solutions these 'experts' proposed for what they saw as the 'Gypsy menace', among which segregation or deportation were popular themes. In 1937, Rohne suggested in the journal *Preussisches und Reichsverwaltungsblatt* setting up special Gypsy quarters in towns, while J. Römer (who also considered that novelists should stop idealising the Gypsies), in *Volk und Rasse*, proposed their deportation to 'lands where they can live easily as nomads' to avoid the danger of their mixing with Germans. The 19 March 1937 edition of the newspaper *NS Land-Post* mentions, presumably with approval, the idea of the Polish Gypsy King Janusz I Kwiek setting up a settlement in Abyssinia. Four years previously District Commissioner Mayerhoffer had urged at a meeting in Oberwart (Austria) that the Gypsies should be deported to Polynesia.

Apart from deportation, the other radical solution was sterilisation. The first recorded mention of this method we have found in Germany dates back to 1937. In that year the journal *Reichsverwaltungsblatt* said that 99 per cent of the Gypsy children in Berleburg were 'ripe for sterilisation'. Discussions in the same year in Hungary of plans to sterilise the Gypsies there also received publicity in the Nazi press.

A concise summary of existing thought in 1939 is provided by Dr Behrendt in an article in *NS Partei Korrespondenz* entitled 'The Truth about the Gypsies':

> They come from India originally and are now a mixed race. There are two million in Europe and North America. In Germany itself 6,000 pure Gypsies live together with 12,000 part-Gypsy or non-Gypsy travellers. The laws of the Gypsies do not permit them to practise birth control. They are criminal and asocial and it is impossible to educate them. All Gypsies should be treated as hereditarily sick.

His solution was the 'elimination without hesitation of this characteristically defective element in the population' and he proposed that this should be done by locking them all up and sterilising them. Rüdiger, too, recommended

their elimination but made no specific proposals. Eva Justin was later to echo
Behrendt's comments by advising that attempts to educate Gypsies should be
abandoned (see below).[3]

THE RACE HYGIENE RESEARCH CENTRE
AND ROBERT RITTER

The origins of German research into Gypsies go back to Alfred Dillmann, a
senior police officer who in 1899 founded an Information Service on Gypsies
in Munich, later called the National Centre for the Fight against the Gypsy
Menace. The main Nazi institution concerned with research into the Gypsies
was established in 1936 by Dr Robert Ritter at the instigation of the Ministry
of the Interior. One year later it became the Race Hygiene and Population
Biology Research Centre of the National Health Office. Ritter and his staff
published numerous writings on the Gypsy question and suggested possible 'solutions'. They were also engaged in drawing up genealogical tables of
German Gypsies and classifying them as being of pure or mixed race. Purity
of race was a Nazi obsession.

The Information Service in Munich already possessed over 18,000 files
on Gypsies when Ritter started work. Some of the persons listed were not,
however, ethnic Gypsies, and others had left Germany. Ritter's intention
was to have every Gypsy in Germany interviewed in order to build lists of
other members of their families and thus to draw up complete genealogical
tables. The aim was to track down every pure and part-Gypsy in the country,
whether they lived in caravans or houses. By February 1941 Ritter had classified 20,000 persons as pure or part-Gypsy. By spring 1942 he said in an
unpublished report that he had 30,000 files, a figure approximately equal to
the total Gypsy population of Greater Germany (including Austria and other
annexed territories).

Announcements concerned with the conscription of women and young
men also indirectly reveal the progress of the classification and tend to bear
out Ritter's claims regarding the numbers of people covered. In 1940 recruit-
ment of women to the Work Service began, but Gypsy and part-Gypsy
women were to be excluded. The Criminal Police were asked to help the
recruiting officers in doubtful cases on the basis of information they had
to hand. If no official classification documents existed then they were to
judge on appearance, manner of life, social position, literacy and so on. Only

especially doubtful cases were to be referred to Ritter's Centre. Thus classification was by no means complete at this date.

In 1941, this time in reference to the call-up of young men for military service, it was stated that all Gypsies should have been classified and the classifications be available in local police stations. Where the experts' decisions were not to hand, the police were asked to inform the Central Police Office (*RKPA*). The classification must then have been almost complete and the researchers not as busy as in the previous year.

By 1944 official circles assumed that all Gypsies would have their classification documents. More importantly, it was noted that no future reference to Gypsies would be made in decrees concerned with the call-up. The unstated reason for this was, as we shall see later, that the majority of the German Gypsies were by then in concentration camps.

Ritter claimed after the war that he stopped working on the subject of Gypsies in 1941, well before the massacre of the German Gypsies. He was never tried. Documents discovered later show that his claim was untrue. One classification statement is dated 1943 and signed by Ritter himself. We shall return again to the subject of his guilt. His views on the Gypsies, part-Gypsies and non-Gypsy Travellers (the Jenische), however, can be found in a number of articles and an unpublished report. Unlike the writers we have previously mentioned, he does make a distinction between pure Romany nomadic Gypsies, whom he would preserve, and part-Gypsies who had often settled in houses. In 1938, in the state health journal *Öffentliche Gesundheitsdienst*, he wrote that Gypsies could not be changed and he returned to this theme again in 1939, when he wrote: 'What is the way to cause this travelling people to disappear? There is no point in making primitive nomads settle and their children go to school.' In this article he says any sexual contact between Gypsies and Germans must be legally forbidden and that the Gypsies of mixed blood should be put in closed work colonies. The pure Gypsies should be given limited areas in which to wander, and winter quarters separate from those of the non-Gypsy Travellers.[4] Then, in his unpublished 1942 report, Ritter stated:

> The Gypsy question can only be considered as solved when the majority of the asocial and useless part-Gypsies have been collected in large camps and set to work, and when the continued procreation of this mixed population is finally prevented. Only then will future generations of the German people be freed from this burden.

His definition of part-Gypsy was very wide:

> A part-Gypsy is a person who has one or two Gypsies among his grand-parents. Further, a person is classed as part-Gypsy if two or more of his grandparents are part-Gypsies as defined above.

This meant that if two of a person's (sixteen) great-great-grandparents were Gypsies he was classed as part-Gypsy and later, from 1943, could be sent to the concentration camp at Auschwitz. Ritter was anxious to hunt out sedentary Gypsies who had merged into society. According to him, many denied they were Gypsies and produced documents such as membership of

FIGURE 3. A worker from Ritter's Centre measures a Gypsy woman's head

the Music Academy or the baptismal certificates of their parents showing that these had a profession. Others had joined the Nazi party, taken up jobs as salesmen or lived in towns. However, with the aid of the genealogical tables he would be able to hunt them out. Later we find that German citizens were encouraged to denounce house-dwelling Gypsies to the police.

Although Ritter did recommend that pure nomadic Gypsies should be allowed to continue travelling under their own laws, none of his other proposals resound to his credit. In our opinion he was as responsible for the large number of Gypsies killed in Germany as were those who carried out the killings. He set up the principle under which a person with one-eighth Gypsy blood counted as a part-Gypsy and insisted that these part-Gypsies represented a danger to established society. Some 18,000 of the German Gypsies were classed as part-Gypsies. In addition, Ritter worked with the police authorities to register all the Gypsies, used threats to obtain information about Gypsies' relations, and is reported to have visited the concentration camps, where survivors said he was treated as if he were a high-ranking Nazi officer.

EVA JUSTIN

After Ritter, Eva Justin was the best known of the racial scientists who concerned themselves with the Gypsies. It has been claimed that when she first visited Gypsy settlements she was thought to be a missionary and was given the Romani nickname 'Loli Tschai' (blond-haired girl) as the Gypsies thought she resembled an earlier missionary (Frieda Zeller) who had that nickname. Later they were surprised to find her behind the interrogation table in the police headquarters when they were called in to be questioned about their families.

In the foreword to her research paper 'The life path of Gypsy children brought up outside their families', published in 1944, she wrote that she hoped it would be a basis for future racial hygiene laws which would prevent any further flow of 'unworthy primitive elements' into the German people. Her paper had studied the history of 148 Gypsy children of mixed race who had been brought up in orphanages or by non-Gypsy foster-parents, and had found, not surprisingly, that the morals of this group were worse than that of a control group brought up in a nomadic tribe — by their own parents! Justin concluded that Gypsies could not be integrated because of their primitive way of thinking. If a Gypsy is educated and remains in the German community, he usually becomes asocial, so all attempts to educate Gypsies and part-Gypsies should stop. The children being brought up in the German community should be sent back to their tribes and socially assimilated adults should be sterilised. 'The German people do not need the multiplying weed of these immature primitives' she wrote, and she concluded her study:

> All educated Gypsies and part-Gypsies of predominantly Gypsy blood, whether socially assimilated or asocial and criminal, should as a general rule be sterilised. Socially integrated part-Gypsies with less than half Gypsy blood can be considered as German . . . Asocial part-Gypsies with less than half Gypsy blood should be sterilised.

After the war, in February 1964, magistrates in Frankfurt decided that there was insufficient evidence to justify a prosecution against Justin. She had taken the theme of her research from Ritter and did not believe in it any more. They accepted that she had not known Gypsies would be sent to concentration camps because of her ideas. Nor could the Gypsy witnesses be sure — after twenty years — that it was Eva Justin who had hit them in a concentration camp.

Ritter himself died in 1950, soon after a legal investigation into his war-time activities had been abandoned. He and the other racial scientists escaped unpunished for their role in the escalation from discrimination to massacre, to which we will now turn.

POLICY FROM 1933

It was evident from the first that there could be no place for nomadic and semi-nomadic Gypsies in the efficient state planned by the Nazis. New laws were enacted and existing legislation strengthened, and many actions were taken against the Gypsies without any legal basis — even within the per-verted system set up by the Nazis.

During the first year of Nazi rule a law for 'the prevention of hereditarily diseased offspring' allowed the sterilisation of some non-Romany Travellers, and other edicts later in the year affected 'asocial' persons. In the following year the expulsion of 'undesirable' foreigners was ordered. Under this law a Gypsy, Agnes Goman, although born in Germany at Duben, was sentenced in 1935 to five days' imprisonment for not having an alien's passport, and then recommended for expulsion. In the same year another Gypsy, Barbara Steinbach, born in Potsdam, and her husband Christian, born in Hanover, were arrested and accused of using a false name. It was said that their real name was Batschuri and they were deported to Hungary.

At an International Police Commission meeting in Copenhagen in 1935 Dr Karl Bader, representing the German police, made no secret of his ideas. He declared:

> The Gypsies, as a foreign element, will never become full members of a host population. Anyone who as a Gypsy disturbs public order and breaks laws should expect no mercy. The solution of this problem lies in the direction of giving an opportunity to all Gypsies and half-Gypsies who wish to conform and work to do so. All others must however be pursued with remorseless rigour and imprisoned or expelled. It might be worth considering including such Gypsies under those persons affected by the law on sterilisation.[5]

In fact the German government was far from 'giving an opportunity to the Gypsies to conform and work'. As non-Aryans they were excluded from schools, the Civil Service and later from the Armed Forces, and restrictions were placed on traditional trades. Richard Rose related:

> In 1937 or 1938 my father was told he could not run his little circus any more. My papers were taken away and I was given special papers so I could no longer work as an acrobat. In 1941 they forced me to work in a factory but two weeks later I was released from the labour corps because I was not pure German.

He was later to end up in Sachsenhausen concentration camp, but survived the 'death march' of prisoners to Wittstock after the camp had been broken up.

Gypsy camps

Small numbers of Gypsies were sent to concentration camps from 1933 but in 1934 the first camp was set up solely for Gypsies and was used for a short period for a group of Scandinavian Gypsies. These had been held on the Dutch–Danish border as they had been refused transit visas to cross Denmark. The Dutch police encouraged them to cross into Germany where they were arrested and held, first in a hostel for the homeless in Altona and then in a locked camp near Bährenfeld. The men were to be set to 'productive work'. This meant carrying pipes several hundred metres, stacking them and then bringing them back to where they had started. The Gypsies were later sent over the border in small groups into Belgium where many of them were to be arrested some years later and sent to Auschwitz.[6]

In many towns permanent caravan sites were set up and Gypsies were forced to live in these special settlements. Among the first were Venloerstrasse in Cologne and Crangerstrasse in Gelsenkirchen, both set up in 1935. Before the Berlin Olympic Games the Gypsies were removed from the capital to a camp set up near Marzahn. The camp was later surrounded by police and dogs and no one was allowed to travel further than Berlin.[7] More residential camps were established in 1937–8.

In 1937 the authorities began to move all the Gypsies in the Frankfurt-am-Main area to a camp in Dieselstrasse. The camp was surrounded by a high wire fence with two policemen on guard, and there were roll calls twice daily. From 1941 the inmates were not allowed to travel and trade, being subjected instead to forced labour; they had to be inside by dusk and the gate was shut until the morning.

Second-class citizens

The Citizenship Law of 1935 distinguished between first-class 'citizens' and second-class 'nationals'. Gypsies were placed in the second class as nationals under this law but lost even this status in April 1943.

Meanwhile, both sedentary and nomad Romanies were being excluded from the German community. The Law for the Protection of German Blood (1935) stated that a marriage could not take place if offspring dangerous to the preservation of the purity of German blood could be expected from it. Dr Brandis, in his commentary on this law, pointed out that it prevented marriages between Germans and either Jews or Gypsies.

Eichwald Rose, part-Gypsy and part-Jewish, was sent to Sachsenhausen concentration camp in June 1938 for having sexual relations with an Aryan girl. He was to be released two years later, after signing a paper agreeing to voluntary sterilisation. Another Gypsy, Franz Klibisch, was sent to a concentration camp for the same reason.[8]

The Decree on the Fight to prevent Crime (1937)

The Decree on the Fight to prevent Crime, passed in 1937, bore particularly upon Gypsies and others classed as 'asocials'. The instructions for carrying out the decree clarified the definition of asocials as including 'those who by anti-social behaviour, even if they have committed no crime, have shown that they do not wish to fit into society, for example, beggars, tramps (Gypsies), prostitutes, and persons with infectious diseases who do not follow treatment.'

Under this decree Gypsies had to sign a declaration that they understood that if they left their place of residence they would be put in a concentration camp. They had to have permanent addresses and stop using the *poste restante* service. Furthermore, they were forbidden to keep cats and dogs. In this early decree the Gypsies are classed together with social groups such as 'beggars, tramps, and persons with infectious diseases who do not follow treatment' but later legislation has racial labels such as 'Jews, Gypsies and Poles'.

In one of the operations following the decree an express letter was sent to every district (*Bezirk*) ordering the police to arrest at least 200 males of working age during the week of 13–18 June 1938 and send them to Buchenwald and other concentration camps. The classes to be arrested included Gypsies and non-Romany Travellers. Gypsies in permanent employment should in theory have been excluded, although in fact in some districts they were taken to make up the numbers. Persons with previous convictions had already been re-arrested on 5 June. One writer, Hans Doering, thinks that, although these measures were taken under the Decree on the Fight to prevent Crime, the real aim was to obtain labour to build concentration camps.

All the males, including youths, were taken from the Gypsy camp in Frankfurt to concentration camps. Some, possibly among those released to celebrate Adolf Hitler's birthday (20 April 1939), later returned, only to be arrested again subsequently. Among the Gypsies imprisoned was a 65-year-old man — Adam Böhmer of the Gypsy camp in Magdeburg. He was accused of being 'work-shy'.

'A.S.' was sent to Sachsenhausen in June 1938 for the same reason and kept there until 1940, when he was released with other Gypsies to work on unexploded bombs.[9] The men from Marzahn camp (Berlin) were also taken to Sachsenhausen.

The Fight against the Gypsy Menace (1938)

In May 1938, on the orders of Heinrich Himmler (Head of the Police), the Munich National Centre for the Fight against the Gypsy Menace was moved to Berlin and made part of the Central Police Office. From then on it would make use of the combined experience of the police and the knowledge gained by the racial scientists, in particular Ritter's Research Centre. The move can be linked with instructions for the police issued by Himmler later that same year.

On 8 December 1938 the combined efforts of the racial scientists and police experts produced the circular *Bekämpfung der Zigeunerplage* (The Fight against the Gypsy Menace). Its racial nature will be clear from the extracts printed below:

A.I.I(1) Experience gained in the fight against the Gypsy menace and the knowledge derived from race-biological research have shown that the proper method of attacking the Gypsy problem seems to be to treat it as a matter of race. It is necessary to treat pure Gypsies and part-Gypsies separately.

(2) To this end it is necessary to establish the racial affinity of every Gypsy living in Germany and also of every vagrant living a Gypsy-like existence.

(3) . . . all settled and non-settled Gypsies, also all vagrants leading a Gypsy-like existence are to be registered with the Centre for the Fight against the Gypsy Menace.

(4) The Police authorities will report all persons who by their looks and appearance, by their customs and habits are to be regarded as Gypsies or part-Gypsies . . .

2(1) . . . An official census is to be taken of all Gypsies, part-Gypsies and vagrants leading a Gypsy-like existence who have passed the age of six.

(2) The nationality has to be entered on the index card. In cases where German or foreign nationality cannot be proved the persons concerned are to be classed as stateless.

3(1) The final decision about the classification of a person as a Gypsy, part-Gypsy or Gypsy-like vagrant will be made by the Criminal Police on the advice of experts.

Instructions for carrying out this decree issued in March 1939 further tightened racial control. Racially pure Gypsies received new brown passes, part-Gypsies light blue passes, and non-Gypsy Travellers grey passes. Under the law nomadic Gypsies were not allowed to stay more than two nights in any one place; the police would tell them where to camp and would separate Gypsy and non-Gypsy travellers. No more foreign Gypsies were to be allowed to enter Germany and those already there were to be expelled. Every police headquarters was to set up a unit for Gypsy problems and one or more persons were to be specifically responsible for Gypsies.

The March 1939 instructions contain this significant paragraph, which indicates the racial nature of the decree:

> The aim of the measures taken by the state must be the racial separation once and for all of the Gypsy race from the German nation, then the prevention of racial mixing and finally the regulation of the conditions of life of the racially pure Gypsies and the part-Gypsy.

An important measure from the authorities' point of view was the registration of the Gypsies. When this had been done it would be possible to see the real numbers involved.

WHEN DID RACIAL PERSECUTION BEGIN?

Much legal argument took place in Germany after 1945 on the question of when racial persecution against the Gypsies began.[10] Many German authorities were concerned to place the date as late as possible in order to cut down on compensation claims. One milestone from the legal viewpoint was the Settlement Decree of October 1939, which prevented the Gypsies from travelling but made no such provision for non-Gypsy nomads. On the other hand, one German court ruled that all the measures taken against the Gypsies up to March 1943 (when they were sent to Auschwitz) were merely 'security measures' and did not amount to racial persecution. We shall leave readers to form their own judgement. We see as a turning point the beginning of the policy of deportation from Germany in 1939, which was later abandoned and replaced by a policy of extermination.

In 1953 the first law was passed in West Germany allowing Gypsies to claim reparations on racial grounds. Then, in 1965, a further law enabled Gypsies to claim for persecution from 1938 onwards. Finally, in August 1981, a new measure was passed in West Germany allowing reparations for survivors who 'are living in hardship' and who had not yet made a claim. This was mainly intended to benefit Jehovah's Witnesses and gay people but also applied to Gypsies who did not fall within the earlier categories of victims. Nevertheless, many survivors of the events we are about to recount never received any compensation.

3

THE ROAD TO AUSCHWITZ

DEPORTATION TO THE EAST

The mere imposition of restrictions on Gypsies did not satisfy the Nazis. It followed logically from the policies applied to Jews and from the views of the racial scientists that they would also want to make Germany free of Gypsies. Reinhard Heydrich, Head of the Security Police, organised a meeting on 21 September 1939 at which it was decided that Gypsies should be sent to recently conquered western Poland. The plan covered all Gypsies in Greater Germany (including recently annexed areas): altogether, a total of 30,000 people. A few categories were in theory to be exempted: those who had been at least five years in regular employment and families in which the mother or father was a non-Gypsy.[11]

It was Heydrich who, less than a month later, issued the Settlement Decree, dated 17 October 1939, under which Gypsies were prohibited from leaving their houses or camping places and had to settle in one place. A count was made in the period 25–27 October and the Gypsies were then collected in special camps until they could be sent to Poland. Meanwhile, the order prevented a Gypsy travelling from place to place even without luggage. To visit relatives at Christmas in 1939 they had to obtain special passes.

The deportations planned for the end of 1939 were postponed, presumably because of a lack of transport, but not for long. At a meeting in Berlin on 30 January 1940, the deportation programme was confirmed.

Heydrich: After the two mass movements (of Jews and Poles) the last mass movement will be the removal of 30,000 Gypsies from Greater Germany to the General Government [i.e. the German-occupied western part of Poland].

Arthur Seyss-Inquart, Deputy Governor of the General Government repeated the figure: 30,000 Gypsies from Germany itself and the (annexed) eastern area.[12]

A special department was created in the Central Security Headquarters — Department IV D 4 (later called IV B 4) — to deal with this deportation of Jews, Gypsies and Poles. Adolf Eichmann was the head of this department. The following exchange was to take place after the end of the war, during the interrogation of Eichmann before his trial for genocide:

Interrogator: The deportation of Gypsies to concentration camps, was this also done by your department IV B 4?

Eichmann: Yes of course . . . not to concentration camps but to ghettos.

Many of the first deportees to Poland were indeed placed in Jewish ghettos, but some 13,000 Gypsies from Greater Germany were later sent to Auschwitz.

The 1940 deportation

The first moves in the planned deportation were initiated by an express letter on 27 April 1940. In the middle of May, the target was for 2,500 Gypsies to be transferred to Poland from the following towns: Hamburg and Bremen (1,000); Cologne, Dusseldorf and Hanover (1,000); and Stuttgart and Frank-furt-am-Main (500).

Certain groups were to be excluded: Gypsies married to Germans or with a father or son in the forces; those who owned land; and anyone with foreign nationality. Persons not able to walk were to be sent to relatives or taken into care. These exemptions compare with similar arrangements for Jews.

Collected together at one point for each area (Hamburg, Cologne and Stuttgart), the Gypsies were then taken on by train, some in cattle trucks and others in normal carriages. The deportation was carried out more or less according to plan and it was intended to carry out further transports. An

FIGURE 4. Deportation from Germany to Poland 1940

official statement speaks of 2,800 Gypsies 'evacuated' to Poland from western Germany during 1940. The extra 300 were a small transport from south Germany which was unloaded in open country, where the Gypsies were left to fend for themselves.

Early in the morning of 16 May 1940 the Gypsies from the Hoherweg internment camp in Dusseldorf were woken from their sleep by the sound of police cars and lorries driving through the camp. Stopfsack, Head of the Dusseldorf Gypsy Department, read out names from a list. Those whose names were called were allowed to pack some clothing, while those on the list who were not in the camp were picked up at their workplaces. They were taken to a collection camp in Cologne, where they had to wait five days while they were checked. During this time they slept in boxes lined with straw. They had to sign that they understood if they returned to Germany they would be sent to a concentration camp although, because the figure of 1,000 for the Cologne area had been exceeded, some of those arrested were allowed to go back to the camp. On 21 May the Gypsies, including 130 from the camp in Hoherweg, were loaded into cattle wagons and taken to Poland. Most of the Dusseldorf deportees were put in the ghetto of Siedlce after the Jews there had been shot or deported to a concentration camp.

Natascha Winter and her family were sent to Sobkow in Poland and put in houses. They were guarded for fourteen days and then this precaution was dropped. Nine months later, with two other families, they made their way back to Karlsruhe, where Natascha had lived before the war. She was later to be taken to Ravensbrück concentration camp.

Apart from the problems of deported Gypsies returning from the east, others wanted to travel east to join relatives. As a general rule it was decided that this would not be permitted. Christian Winterstein of Worms was, however, given permission to go if he paid for his own transport. The General Government authorities wrote to Berlin in November 1940 saying they did not want relatives to come, at least for the present, as the situation was already chaotic. They thought it might be possible to admit them after April of the following year. Late in 1941, however, an order forbade Gypsies to travel to the General Government.

Prior to this, in October 1940, when nearly 27,000 Gypsies remained in Germany and Austria, it had been decided to stop further deportations to Poland. Various reasons have been put forward to explain the halt: transport was needed for war purposes; Governor Frank of Poland objected as he was trying to organise the country efficiently; the classification of Gypsies was not yet complete. In addition, priority was being given to the expulsion of the Jews, as their flats were needed for Germans returning from the Russian-occupied Baltic states. A combination of these reasons probably led to the decision. Deportation was, however, still the solution envisaged to the so-called Gypsy problem, although it might have to be postponed until after the expected victory in the war. At a meeting in Prague in November 1941 it was suggested that the German Gypsies could be deported to Riga but nothing came of this.

DISMISSED FROM THE ARMED FORCES

Although Gypsies should in theory have been excluded from the army by law as early as November 1937, many classified as pure and part-Gypsy were still serving at the beginning of the Second World War. Some had even received medals. Early in 1941 the army authorities reaffirmed that on the grounds of racial policy no more Gypsies and part-Gypsies should be called up. Those in the army were to be placed in reserve units and no further medals were to be awarded to Gypsies. The police sent lists of the persons concerned to the army. In the same month a secret order went out that Gypsies should not be employed in munitions factories and other top security institutions.[13]

Gypsies were released from the air force by a decree dated 7 January 1942 and, later in the year, from the navy and the army. Those from the latter listed as part-Gypsies were enrolled in the Second Reserve of the Territorial Army. The release of servicemen took some time and Gypsies could still be found in the army as late as 1943.

THE PRESSURE MOUNTS

After November 1939 Gypsies received special work-cards and in many cases their other papers were taken away from them. Richard Rose found that with this new work-card he was unable to continue as a circus artist.

In March 1942 Gypsies found themselves placed on the same footing as the Jews with regard to labour laws. Under these regulations they lost the right to sickness and holiday pay. Those listed as part-Gypsy with at least half Gypsy blood were to be classed as Gypsies for the purposes of these laws. From April Gypsies had to relinquish 15 per cent of their income as a special tax. This already applied to Poles but not, until later, to Jews. A further restriction forbade the Gypsies to travel to Berlin.

The marriage laws were reaffirmed and strengthened. A secret order from the Minister of the Interior said that 'since Gypsies endanger the purity of the German blood' careful attention must be given to requests by them to marry. Even Gypsies with less than a quarter Gypsy blood must not be allowed to marry Germans.

Discrimination in the field of education had already started in the pre-war years. Back in 1936 an edict of the Ministry of the Interior said that research should be carried out into whether Gypsies were fit for education and whether Gypsy orphans should be fostered. As we have seen above, the racial scientists supplied the desired negative answers.

In Cologne after February 1939 only one class existed for all the Gypsy children in the town, and the Frankfurt Gypsies were dismissed from school in 1941 'because of the shortage of teachers'. Those who did attend had to put up with persecution by other children. Olga Owczarek remembers that she was driven out by the other children who hit her and her brother and shouted, 'You Gypsy bandits and Jews, get out of our school.' The Ministry of Education announced in March 1941 that persons without citizenship could not attend school. Gypsies lacking German nationality were excluded and the police were instructed to expel from the country any of them who became a 'social nuisance' as a result of having no occupation. Gypsy children holding German nationality had the theoretical right to attend classes. However, 'if they were a moral or other danger to the German children' they should be dismissed and the police informed.[14]

CLASSIFICATION

In view of its importance in future legislation we give here a brief account of the different groups of Gypsies in Germany, using the classification set up by the racial scientists in 1939.

The 'Sinti' had come as early as the fifteenth century and could be called native to Germany. There were 13,000 in 1939, many of them musicians. The name perhaps came from the province of Sindh in India. The 'Lalleri', a smaller group, numbered some 1,000 when counted in 1942. The 'Roma' had come to Germany from Hungary in 1860–70 and were mainly horse-dealers. In 1940 there were 1,800. Other groups included some 8,000 'Balkan Gypsies' in the Austrian Burgenland, 2,000 'Litautikker' in East Prussia, and smaller groups — Drisari, Kelderari, Lovari, Medvashi (bear trainers), Yugoslav Gypsies, and basket-makers, who together probably numbered fewer than 1,000.

The first hint of any distinction in law between different Gypsy groups came in August 1941 when a refinement of an earlier division into pure and part-Gypsy was set up:

Z [*Zigeuner*]	pure Gypsy
ZM+, ZM(+)[*Zigeunermischling*]	more than half-Gypsy
ZM	part-Gypsy
ZM 1st grade	half-Gypsy, half-German
ZM 2nd grade	one parent ZM 1st grade, one parent German
ZM-, ZM(-)	more than half-German
NZ [Nicht-Zigeuner]	non-Gypsy

In addition, Gypsies of the Sinti group were to be noted as 'native Gypsies' (*Inländische Zigeuner*).

The Central Police Office was to decide the treatment to be applied to classes ZM- and ZM(-) under the various laws, but we doubt whether such a detailed classification as the above was ever carried out for the majority of German Gypsies. Such documents as we have seen indicate 'predominantly Gypsy blood' or similar phrases, and the classification was not based entirely on genealogy. Ritter explained that he divided Gypsies into pure and mixed on the following grounds:

1. General impression and physical appearance
2. Belonging to a Romani-speaking community
3. Links with tribal law
4. Gypsy way of life
5. Genealogy

TOWARDS ANNIHILATION

Deportations to the East were abandoned as the Nazis fell upon a simpler solution to the Gypsy problem. They had been gassing mentally handicapped Germans for some time and had learnt from this experience. A mass murder of Jews had taken place at Treblinka in December 1940, an experimental gassing station was established at Auschwitz in September 1941 and the first permanent gassing camp was set up at Chelmno in December that year. Some sources suggest that the decision to annihilate the Jews had already been made as early as June 1941. Certainly, a conference at Wannsee on 20 January 1942 marked its definite acceptance. Later in the same year, the policy was extended to Gypsies.

It has not been established with certainty who made the decision to annihilate the Gypsies alongside the Jews. The available evidence points to a personal decision by Himmler. Other Nazi leaders were, of course, involved in the discussions leading to the policy, and thought would also have been given to the Gypsies in conquered lands. Prior to a planned eventual invasion of Britain, the Central Security Headquarters (Department VI D 7b) tried to get information about Gypsies living in Great Britain, as the following correspondence reveals. The letters were sent to the police attachés in Sweden and Spain and to Holland:

Berlin. 14.viii.1942

Nr 66558/42 Secret.

Precisions about the Gypsies living in Great Britain. You are asked to use all your contacts to establish the number of Gypsies living in Great Britain. We are also interested in the British Gypsy Laws and the way in which the Gypsies in Britain are regarded and treated (military service, freedom of movement, restrictions etc.). When parachutists and other prisoners from Great Britain are interrogated I ask you to add this question. You are asked to give the matter the utmost priority.

Signed Dr Schambacher

The only reply we have found was most unhelpful to the Nazis:

Hague. 15.viii.1942
The prisoners in Haaren camp have been carefully questioned. They declare unanimously that they have never seen Gypsies travelling during their stay in England. Some prisoners who were in England before the war declared that they never saw any Gypsies even then apart from the Gypsy orchestras in night clubs and so on. One prisoner had seen a film in which a Gypsy King living in Yorkshire was shown. The same prisoner said he had also met Gypsies in the Pioneer Corps.[15]

On 18 September 1942 there was a meeting at Himmler's field headquarters. This was attended by Himmler himself, Otto Thierack (Minister of Justice), Curt Rothenburger (Justice Ministry), Bruno Streckenbach (Central Police Headquarters) and Bender (a legal expert from the SS). The meeting decided that 'Persons under protective arrest, Jews, Gypsies and Russians . . . would be delivered by the Ministry of Justice to the SS to be worked to death.'[16]

The SS (*Schutzstaffel*) was a para-military organisation which had worked for the Nazi Party rather than the government and ran the concentration camps. This decision referred to Jews, Gypsies and Russians who were already under arrest, and extended a 1939 agreement. A letter from Thierack to Martin Bormann (Head of the Nazi Party) dated 13 October read:

With the intention of liberating the German area from Poles, Russians, Jews and Gypsies . . . I envisage transferring all criminal proceedings

concerning [these people] to Himmler. I do this because I realise that
the courts can only feebly contribute to the extermination of these
people . . . There is no point in keeping these people for years in prison.
I ask you to let me know if the Führer approves of this way of thinking.
If so, I will in due course present plans through Dr Hans Lammers.
[Hans Lammers was Hitler's legal adviser.]

About 12,000 persons, including Gypsies, were affected by this plan.
It amounted to a request for authority from Hitler to carry out what had
already been decided between Himmler and Thierack, to move members of
these groups from prisons to concentration camps. It would seem, however,
that a decree of August 1942 had already given Thierack power to do this on
his own initiative. On 9 October, four days earlier than the above letter, it
had already been announced that any Jews, Gypsies, Russians and Ukrainians who were serving sentences in prison as asocial persons were to be handed
over to the authority of the Head of the SS (Himmler). Gypsy women were
to be included. Foreign Gypsies were not to be classed as foreign and were
therefore also to be handed over.

By 5 November 1942, Thierack's proposition had been approved by
Hitler.[17] Jews and Gypsies in prison were to be handed over to the SS. For
those outside prison the same fate awaited them in due course.

HIMMLER'S PLAN FOR THE 'PURE' GYPSIES

It is clear that some time in 1942 Himmler had decided Gypsies as a whole
were to be annihilated.[18] However, he stated more than once that he wished
to preserve two groups, the so-called 'pure' Sinti and the Lalleri. Other leaders must have known about this intention, because on 14 September 1942
Joseph Goebbels (Propaganda Minister) is reported as telling Thierack that
in his opinion all nomads should be exterminated without any distinction
between one group and another.

Himmler went as far as making the necessary preparations for organising these two groups. Nine representatives were appointed on 13 October
that year by the Central Police Office, eight for the Sinti and one for the
Lalleri. The eight Sinti were supposed to work through their local police
headquarters while the Lalleri spokesman was responsible to the police in
Berlin. Allowed to travel freely, they were to make lists of those to be saved.
In the case of the Sinti these included part-Gypsies whom they considered

could be attached to the tribes of pure Sinti (as established by Ritter and his team). The racial scientists considered that there were no pure Lalleri and the latter's spokesman, Gregor Lehmann, was to make a list of those Lalleri Gypsies whom he believed could be formed into a tribal group and be permitted to follow a nomadic life.[19]

The Lalleri had previously been classed as foreign Gypsies in an edict of August 1941. By October 1942 the Lalleri had been reclassified as 'native' Gypsies, a classification already given to the Sinti. A passage in an article by Ritter gives a clue as to why the change was made:

> The Lalleri came from the German-speaking part of Bohemia and Moravia in earlier centuries. Most of them belonged to a tribe which was living in the Sudetenland when it was annexed to Germany.

Thus the fact they had lived for some years among German-speaking people qualified them for preservation, although they were acknowledged to be of mixed race. If the opinions of the racial scientists had been followed to a logical conclusion, the mixed-race Lalleri would have been seen as a greater menace than the pure Kelderari and Balkan Gypsies. The fact that they formed a small, easily controlled and homogeneous group must have influenced the decision. The writer Reimar Gilsenbach thought that the total to be saved would have been between 200 and 300.

When Bormann found out — via Arthur Nebe of the Criminal Police — about Himmler's intentions to exempt two tribes he wrote on 3 December 1942 to the SS Chief:

> Through my expert's conversation with Nebe, I have been informed that the treatment of the so-called pure Gypsies is going to have new regulations. They are going to keep their language, lore and customs in use and be allowed to travel around freely. In certain cases they will serve in special units of the army. All this because they have in general not behaved in an asocial manner, and in their system of belief they have preserved valuable Germanic customs. I am of the opinion that the conclusions of your expert are exaggerated and unlikely. Such a special treatment would mean a fundamental deviation from the simultaneous measures for fighting the Gypsy menace and would not be understood at all by the population and the lower leaders of the party. Also the Führer would not agree to give one section of the Gypsies their old freedom. The facts have been

unknown to me up to now and seem also to be unlikely. I would like to be informed about this. As soon as possible.[20]

No reply to this letter has been found. Discussion on the settlement of so-called pure Gypsies and Gypsy research in general took up thirty-five minutes of a meeting on 10 February 1943 in the Central Police Office attended by its director Nebe and, from Ahnenerbe (an institution founded by the SS in 1939 to investigate the heritage of the 'Nordic Indo-Germanic' race), Wolfram Sievers. Plans must still have been vague. The original suggestion was apparently to settle the two exempted tribes in the Ödenburg (Sopron) district but as this was part of Hungary it could only remain an idea. Why Himmler had proposed in October 1942 to let these groups wander freely throughout Germany we cannot be sure. Advocates of the plan said they were no danger to German racial purity as they did not marry non-Gypsies. Yet it had been stated that 90 per cent of the Sinti and all the Lalleri were the result of mixed marriages. No attempt was made to select pure Sinti or other groups in the other countries under Nazi domination. This suggests Himmler's sole aim must have been to preserve a limited number for study purposes through Ahnenerbe.

THE AUSCHWITZ DECREE

On 16 December 1942, Himmler signed a decree which ordered the sending of the Gypsies of Germany to Auschwitz. This order referred to the Internment of Gypsies of mixed race, Rom Gypsies and Balkan Gypsies in the concentration camp. This was swiftly followed by a series of other Auschwitz decrees applying to Gypsies from occupied countries in the west, suggesting in our view that a decision had been taken in 1942 to wipe out the Gypsies throughout Europe. The Ministry of the Interior ruled (in the Confiscation Decree of 25 January 1943) that the property of Gypsies sent to concentration camps should be confiscated. This was partly to avoid the confusion of the 1940 deportations, when piles of clothing were left for the deportees' relatives to collect.

Four days later (29 January), Himmler circulated instructions for carrying out his orders concerning Auschwitz. All Rom Gypsies as well as part-Gypsies belonging to the Sinti clan were to be sent to the concentration camp in March 1943. The pure Sinti and the Lalleri were exempted, together with those classed as Sinti part-Gypsies who could be attached to the nomadic

Reichssicherheitshauptamt   Berlin, am 29. Januar 1943
V A 2 Nr. 59/43 g

Schnellbrief

An

die Leiter der Kriminalpolizeileitstellen — oder Vertreter im Amt —
(ausgenommen KPLStelle Wien),

nachrichtlich an

a) den Leiter der Partei-Kanzlei in München, Braunes Haus:
b) den Reichsführer-ƆƆ, Reichskommissar für die Festigung deutschen
   Volkstums, in Berlin;
c) alle Höheren ƆƆ- und Polizeiführer (ausgenommen Wien, Salzburg.
   Metz, Krakau, Oslo, Den Haag, Belgrad, Riga, Kiew, Rußland Mitte.
   Paris und z. b. V.);

[...]

Betrifft: **Einweisung von Zigeunermischlingen, Róm-Zigeunern und bal-
           kanischen Zigeunern in ein Konzentrationslager**

Anlagen: Drei.

I. Auf Befehl des Reichsführers-ƆƆ vom 16. 12. 1942 — Tgb. Nr. I
2652/42 Ad./RF/V — sind Zigeunermischlinge, Róm-Zigeuner und nicht
deutschblütige Angehörige zigeunerischer Sippen balkanischer Herkunft
nach bestimmten Richtlinien auszuwählen und in einer Aktion von
wenigen Wochen in ein Konzentrationslager einzuweisen. Dieser Per-
sonenkreis wird im Nachstehenden kurz als „zigeunerische Personen"
bezeichnet.

Die Einweisung erfolgt ohne Rücksicht auf den Mischlingsgrad fami-
lienweise in das Konzentrationslager (Zigeunerlager) Auschwitz.

Die Zigeunerfrage in den Alpen- und Donau-Reichsgauen wurde durch
besonderen Erlaß geregelt.

Die künftige Behandlung der reinrassigen Sinte- und der als reinrassig geltenden Lalleri-Zigeuner-Sippen bleibt einer späteren Regelung
vorbehalten.

II. **Von der Einweisung bleiben ausgenommen:**

1. Reinrassige Sinte- und Lalleri-Zigeuner;

2. Zigeunermischlinge, die im zigeunerischen Sinne gute Mischlinge sind
   u. gem. Erlaß des Reichssicherheitshauptamtes vom 13. 10. 1942 — V A 2
   Nr. 2260/42 — und vom 11. 1. 43 — V A 2 Nr. 40/43 — einzelnen reinrassigen Sinte- und als reinrassig geltenden Lalleri-Zigeunersippen
   zugeführt werden;

3. zigeunerische Personen, die mit Deutschblütigen rechtsgültig ver-
   heiratet sind;

4. sozial angepaßt lebende zigeunerische Personen, die bereits vor der
   allgemeinen Zigeunererfassung in fester Arbeit standen und feste
   Wohnung hatten.
   Die Entscheidung, ob eine zigeunerische Person sozial angepaßt
   lebt, hat die zuständige Kriminalpolizei(leit)stelle auf Grund polizei-
   licher Feststellungen und erforderlichenfalls nach Einholung der
   Stellungnahmen der zuständigen Dienststellen der NSDAP. (Kreis-
   leiter. NSV., Rassenpolitisches Amt) zu treffen. Zu berücksichtigen
   sind auch die Beurteilung durch den Arbeitgeber und die Aus-
   kunft der zuständigen Krankenkasse.
   Bei allen wandergewerbetreibenden zigeunerischen Personen ist die
   Frage der sozialen Anpassung zu verneinen, es sei denn, daß sie nach-
   weisbar eigene Erzeugnisse vertreiben.

5. zigeunerische Personen, die auf Anordnung des Reichskriminalpolizei-
   amtes aus den für Zigeuner geltenden Bestimmungen herausgenom-
   men sind;

6. zigeunerische Personen, die noch zum Wehrdienst eingezogen sind
   oder im gegenwärtigen Krieg als versehrt oder mit Auszeichnungen
   aus dem Wehrdienst entlassen wurden;

7. zigeunerische Personen, deren Herausnahme aus dem Arbeitseinsatz
   durch die zuständige Rüstungsinspektion oder durch das Arbeitsamt
   aus wehrwirtschaftlichen Gründen abgelehnt wird:

8. Ehegatten und die nicht wirtschaftlich selbständigen Kinder der vor-
   stehend unter 3—7 aufgeführten zigeunerischen Personen:

9. zigeunerische Personen, bei denen nach Auffassung der zuständigen
   Kriminalpolizei(leit)stelle die Einweisung in das Zigeunerlager aus
   besonderen Gründen zunächst auszusetzen ist;

Der ursprüngliche Geheimcharakter ist gemäß VI 13 obigen Erlasses mit
Wirkung vom 1. 5. 1943 aufgehoben.

FIGURE 5. The order to carry out Himmler's Auschwitz Decree

tribes. Some other categories were also left out theoretically (but not in practice), namely: Gypsies married to Germans; socially assimilated Gypsies with settled work and accommodation; Gypsies still in the army or who had been released with decorations or wounded; those needed in factories; spouses and dependent children of the above; and foreign citizens.

Gypsies with court convictions and those who had broken the Settlement Decree of 1939 by continuing to behave as nomads were to be sent to Auschwitz even if they belonged to exempted categories. The police would encourage the exempted Gypsies, other than foreign citizens, to be sterilised. If they refused there were provisions for their compulsory sterilisation.

When the police rounded up Gypsies they in fact took little notice of the exceptions listed above. Several cases are known of Gypsies married to Germans being sent to Auschwitz while reports from the camp speak of others arriving still wearing military decorations on their clothes. They should not have been there and we must conclude that practice was very different from theory. Gypsies were taken from the Daimler-Benz factory although the foreman wanted to keep them. Though Ferdinand Kraus was in Nazi terms 'socially assimilated' and even a member of the Nazi Party, he was persecuted as a Gypsy.[21] There is ample evidence that foreign Gypsies did not escape either. In December 1942 two officials, Westphal and Erhardt, had been made responsible for seeing that they were handed over to the police.

No mention is made in the law of the smaller tribes (Medvashi and others). We can assume that they were taken to the camps with the rest. The vast majority of those sent to Auschwitz had been classified as part-Gypsies and belonged to the Sinti tribe. The lists of exempted Sinti and Lalleri were supposed to be ready before the transports to Auschwitz began. But only three of the nine 'spokesmen' had compiled their lists by 11 January 1943 — Gregor Lehmann, Karl Weiss and one other.[22] Heinrich Steinberg refused to write a list because his wife and son were already in concentration camps. Gregor Lehmann had travelled to annexed Moravska-Ostrava to seek out Lalleri, and survivors claim that he took bribes from persons who wanted to be put on the lists. Arrested after the war, he was handed over to the Russians and sentenced to a term in prison.

Himmler ordered the completed lists to be sent to local police stations and checked immediately. Any Gypsies with criminal records were crossed off, together with members of their families. The police had orders to be especially strict if the lists were long. Only Lalleri Gypsies proposed by the Lalleri spokesman could be admitted to the lists, and the police were to make lists for the areas where the Sinti spokesmen had not done so. Many of the exempted Sinti would have been sedentary, not nomadic, which seems to contradict the whole point of the law and the recommendations of the racial scientists to separate Gypsies from Germans.

Most of this activity proved to be a futile blind. When the police came to collect the Gypsies at Magdeburg and from a camp near Neubranden-burg they took away everyone. This undoubtedly happened elsewhere. Josef Langryn was on the Lalleri list but still had to join Organisation Todt, a labour brigade. He fled and on recapture was sent back to the unit to be put on trial for 'cowardice before the enemy'. He was probably shot.[23]

The Citizenship Law as amended in April 1943 gave no status to the exempted Gypsies, probably because they were to be sent out of Germany after the war. A decree was passed on 27 March 1943 declaring that those classified as pure were to be excused from Labour Service and military enlistment. Part-Gypsies were to serve in the Second Reserve. This is the last official use of the term 'pure Gypsies'. Further round-ups of German Gypsies had in any case already begun.

FIGURE 6. Deportation from Germany to Auschwitz, 1943

DEPORTATION TO AUSCHWITZ

The first transport had arrived at Auschwitz on 26 February 1943, even before a special camp for the Gypsies had been built. Following this, nearly 10,000 German Gypsies arrived in Auschwitz within a few weeks and the new camp was overflowing. Many others, of course, had already been imprisoned in Sachsenhausen and other camps. A few Gypsies may have survived through their status as 'pure' Sinti, while others continued to live under supervision outside the camps.

On 8 March 1943 at 5 A.M. six Gestapo men came to the flat of Josef H. in Munich. He, his wife and their six children were put on a lorry and taken to the Police Headquarters in Ettstrasse where they were put in a communal cell. On that day 136 Gypsies in all were arrested in Munich. On 13 March they were taken, again by lorry, to the station and loaded into cattle trucks. After five days with little food or water, they arrived at Auschwitz and were driven with blows into the camp.

Some Gypsies were even taken away from their place of employment and sent away without their family having any idea of what had happened to them. Each authority made its own interpretation of the general order. Some separated the parents from their children by taking the parents into the camps and leaving the children behind or vice versa.

Reports from different towns indicated that, to avoid incidents, the Gypsies were told they were going to be resettled in Poland. The authorities promised each would be given a horse, a pig and a cow. While Jews were seized by the Security Police (SD), the arrests of Gypsies were carried out by the police (Kripo): the ordinary police held the lists of Gypsies and it was more convenient for them to handle the deportations.

Pitzo Adler continued working in a factory until November 1944. He was then drafted into a Home Guard unit but dismissed again because of his race. He was sent to the main camp at Auschwitz and died there. Three other men were still working in an ammunition factory in spring 1945 and their families had the special privilege of being allowed to shelter in the toilets of an air-raid shelter. Other Gypsies are known to have been working in the coal mines up to December 1944.

As described above, Germans were encouraged to denounce Gypsies to the police. Thus, Margarete Dickow wrote in June 1943 to the Gypsy Office of the Berlin Police pointing out two Gypsies, Johann Krause and Heinrich

Freiwald and their families. As no action was taken, she wrote again in October asking for some effort to be made so that the Gypsies and their children would be arrested and removed to a camp. Until then those Gypsies had been classed as Germans.[24]

Gypsy children were weeded out of orphanages and hospitals. Police Officer Schulz-Lenhardt of Magdeburg wrote in November 1943 to the

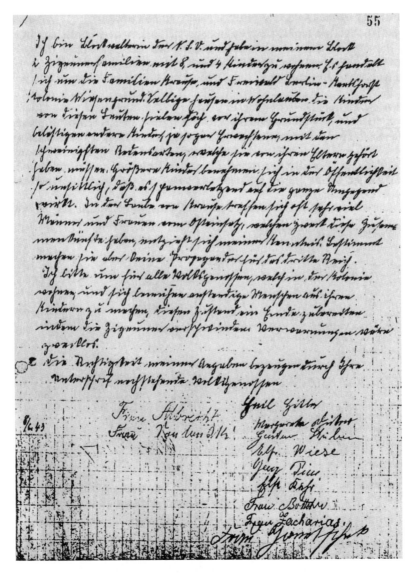

FIGURE 7. Letter denouncing a Gypsy family

National Centre for the Fight against the Gypsy Menace, then in Fursten-burg-Mecke, saying he had discovered three Gypsy children in an orphanage at Schonebeck on the Elbe. Excusing himself for not having found them and sent them to Auschwitz earlier, he asked the Centre what he should do. Two weeks later the police dispatched them to the concentration camp. The children were Christel Rose, Loni Steinbach and Seppel Tritschler. Christel was ten at the time.

In 1938 all the Gypsy children in care in Wurttemberg state had been brought together in one children's home, St Joseph's in Mulfingen. It seems that they were not immediately sent to Auschwitz, as Eva Justin was studying them. Shortly after she had completed her research in 1944 all forty were sent to Auschwitz. Many were dead even by the time her thesis was published later that year. By the end of the war only four still survived.

The scheme to preserve a group of Sinti and Lalleri was now definitely forgotten. By March 1944 the number of Gypsies remaining free was so small that Himmler issued the following notice:

> As far as Jews, Poles and Gypsies are concerned, the accomplished evacu-ation of these groups by the Chief of Police has made the publication of special decrees for them meaningless.

Well over half of the Gypsies living in Germany perished during the Nazi period.

EUROPE UNDER THE NAZIS:

OCCUPIED COUNTRIES IN THE WEST

We turn now to the territories occupied and largely administered by the Germans: in this chapter, the occupied countries in the west — Austria and other annexed territories, the Czech lands, Belgium, Denmark, France, Holland, Luxembourg and Norway.

AUSTRIA

The Nazi leaders in Austria were determined to take harsh measures against the Gypsies. As early as 1938, Tobias Portschy, the Nazi leader in Steiermark (Burgenland), sent an oft-cited memorandum to Dr Lammers, Chief of the Chancellery, of which one passage is enough to indicate its tone:

> Because the Gypsies have manifestly a heavily tainted heredity and because they are inveterate criminals who constitute parasites in the bosom of our people, it is fitting in the first place to watch them closely, to prevent them from reproducing themselves and to subject them to the obligation of forced labour in labour camps.[25]

A letter in a similar vein from Dr Meissner, General Public Prosecutor in Graz, in 1940, recommended sterilisation of all Gypsies in the Burgenland. As it is not so well known, we give a longer extract here:

> The Gypsies, especially in the district of the lower court of Oberwarth where about 4,000 of them live, are a danger, less from the political than

43

from the racial and economic point of view. Among them the pure bred (black) Gypsies probably constitute the majority. They subsist almost exclusively by begging and stealing. Their activities as musicians represent more a camouflage than a means of earning a living. Their existence is an extraordinarily great burden for the honest working population, especially the farmers whose fields they plunder, a burden growing from year to year . . . The mass of the Gypsies still resemble externally primitive African or Asiatic peoples . . . Interbreeding with this morally and spiritually inferior people will necessarily mean a decrease in the value of the offspring. On the other hand interbreeding is encouraged by the fact that the young Gypsy men are especially sexually aggressive while the Gypsy girls are sexually unrestrained . . . It is not possible to fight this danger by guarding them in central camps. Their transfer to a foreign country, too, is hardly possible. Since they have no means of subsistence they cannot be deprived of it. They are (now) German nationals and will of course be rejected without consideration by any other country. The only effective way I can see of relieving the population of the Burgenland from this nuisance . . . is the universal sterilisation of all Gypsies . . . These wandering work-shy beings of alien race will never become faithful to the State and will always endanger the moral level of the German population.[26]

Austria had been annexed to Germany in 1938 and Nazi-inspired action against the Jews and the 10,000 Austrian Gypsies had started almost immediately. Two months after Austria's absorption into the Reich, it was announced on 4 May 1938 that Gypsies would be treated as they were in Germany. A few days later Himmler ordered the fingerprinting of the entire Gypsy community and forbade them to leave the country. Gypsy children were removed from schools in some Protestant parishes and sporadic arrests began. From October it was decreed that relatives of interned Gypsies would be disqualified from receiving welfare aid.

Some of the first arrests occurred on 22 June, when German officials came to Stegersbach. They intended to take several Gypsies and as one of those on the list was away they took instead a man named Adolf Gussak who worked for the local priest and lived in his house. Taken to Dachau, he found that conditions were already bad and rules were made to make life a burden for the Austrian and German Gypsies there. They were made to wear

FIGURE 8. Deportation from Austria, 1938

coats when it was hot and leave them off in the cold. The guards forced them to crawl and bark like dogs and to sleep under their beds. In March 1939 Gussak was transferred to Mauthausen concentration camp where, on one occasion, he received twenty-five lashes as a punishment for writing to the priest, his former employer. He survived the war, although his wife was to die in Ravensbrück.

That first autumn the government of the district of Burgenland ordered that all Gypsy men and women fit for labour should be forced into agricultural work wherever there was a need. Work-camps were later set up in Vienna, in the Tyrol and elsewhere. Then, early in June 1939, a decree ordered between 2,000 and 3,000 Gypsy adults to be arrested and sent to concentration camps in Germany. This move was similar to action taken in Germany the previous summer (when Gypsies had been sent to Ravensbrück and Dachau). Conditions in the camps were so poor that many had already succumbed to disease and starvation in the first winter.

The policy established in September 1939 was that the Austrian Gypsies should be deported to the east, together with those from Germany, in order to make the country Gypsy-free. In April 1940 it was arranged to send the largest group, those living in the Burgenland, to Poland. The local authorities in other districts, however, planned to use the opportunity to rid themselves of Gypsies by dispatching them all to the Burgenland, from where they would be transported eastwards; as a result it was later decided to send them from each district. Finally, the whole scheme fell through. An express letter dated 31 October 1940 announced that the 'resettlement' of 6,000 Austrian Gypsies to Poland was to be delayed 'because after the war another solution of the Gypsy problem is envisaged'.

In October 1939 Heydrich had ordered that Gypsies in Greater Germany (Germany and Austria) should be registered and put in internment camps, from which they would not be allowed to move, in preparation for deportation to German-occupied Poland. A number of internment camps were set up. One such camp was in Salzburg (Maxglan), and held 110 Gypsies in 1939 and 160 in 1940. The inmates were transferred to a camp in the stables of the Salzburg race-track ready for deportation. However, when the deportation was called off they were returned to Maxglan with other Gypsies from the region. Two large barracks surrounded by a two-metre-high barbed-wire fence were erected for the 300 prisoners, and the camp had an armed guard. Food was poor and freedom restricted. The inmates had to work on the roads and in agriculture, and about fifty prisoners were sent for a few weeks to act as extras in the director Leni Riefenstahl's film *Tiefland*. Wages for this and other work were paid into a communal fund to cover those unable to work. Between January and April 1943 the majority of prisoners were sent to Auschwitz. The remainder went to Lackenbach and the Salzburg camp was closed.

Gypsies from Innsbruck, Klagenfurt and Linz were assembled in collection camps and similar arrangements were made for the 6,000 Gypsies from Vienna and Burgenland. These Gypsies, who for several generations had been sedentary except for summer migrations, were now faced with eviction from their homes. Settlements containing less than fifty persons were broken up and the inhabitants moved to larger ones. Communal kitchens served meals and 90 per cent of earnings were taken for communal expenditure. Many men were allocated to work-camps at Linz and Eisenerz.

Lackenbach

The camp at Lackenbach, set up the previous year, was expanded in 1941 and between 3,000 and 4,000 Gypsies passed through there in total. This camp was for Gypsies only and, in 1941, there were mass transports of Austrian Gypsies to the camp. Because Lackenbach came under the Criminal Police and not the SS it was never officially classified as a concentration camp, but conditions hardly differed. No high-voltage electric fence was built but the usual roll-calls, corporal punishment and forced labour went on. The prisoners were permitted, however, to stay in family groups. Rosalia Karoly was one of the internees:

> On a Sunday in August 1941 we were collected by the police and sent to Lackenbach. I was twelve. On the following day I was sent to work digging a canal. I was already beaten on the first day. My mother was beaten with a rubber truncheon by Camp Commander Langmuller.

Josef Hodoschi was sent to Lackenbach on 19 September 1941. He escaped but was recaptured, returned to the camp and given twenty-five strokes with the rubber truncheon. His mother and siblings all died at Auschwitz. Another survivor, Franz Karall, recalls that both the Camp Commander and a Gypsy Kapo, Alexander Sarkozi, ran through the camp with whips and beat anyone they wished.

Johann Knobloch, an Austrian who was allowed to visit the camp in the spring of 1943 to obtain specimens of Romani dialects, has provided a description of the conditions:

> The Gypsy Camp at Lackenbach was under the control of the Security Police (SD). The main part of the camp consisted of three long barracks each of which was divided by a corridor into two halves. In these halves further divisions created smaller rooms, which gave enough space to the inhabitants. One barrack was intended for the Sinti, one for the Rom and one for those of mixed race . . . I discovered that efforts were being made to set up a Gypsy genealogy. I asked the purpose of this work and was told that it was intended to stop marriage between those of mixed race and further mixing. When I asked if it was intended to keep the Gypsies in the camps for ever I was told this was only a necessity because of the war and that after the war the Gypsies would be able to continue their nomadic life again and earn their living as previously by music and other activities. In fact there was an orchestra in the camp that had played once during an inspection by higher authorities from Vienna.
>
> Apart from this, the men were occupied in two work parties, one building roads and the other felling trees in the forest. There was also a teacher in the camp (Mrs Wajbele) who taught the children. She was a Gypsy and asked me for pencils . . . The spokesmen enjoyed a superior position in the camp. For the Sinti 'Lumpo' Schneeberger was the

spokesman and for the Rom of the Burgenland Alexander Sarkozi. The food in the camp was not bad, of course there was also horse-meat which the Gypsies avoid when they are free to do so.[27]

At his trial after the war Langmuller was accused of responsibility for 287 deaths. In one incident thirty-five to forty children were poisoned, possibly deliberately but more probably during some medical experiment. Sarkozi also faced trial.

The Nazi authorities in Austria regarded the prisoners in Lackenbach as being on the same level as those in concentration camps. Karl Gerland, the Deputy Head of the district of Lower Austria, was to offer them to Himmler for use in medical experiments. Those who died from the poor food and lack of medical attention were buried in the neighbouring Jewish graveyard.

Deportation to Lodz

The deportation programme for Austria reopened in 1941 when five transports of 5,000 persons in all were sent to Lodz Ghetto. Internees from Lackenbach made up 2,000 of that total. Others were sent from Furstenfeld, Hartberg, Mattersburg, Oberwart and Roter Thurm. As we recount later (in Chapter 7), only a handful from these transports survived.

To Auschwitz

Finally, late in 1942 preparations were made for the extermination of the remaining Austrian Gypsies. Anton Schneeberger was set up as representative of the Austrian Sinti, to make a list of so-called pure Sinti who would be spared. Apparently no such list was ever made.[28] The order to send the Austrian Gypsies to Auschwitz came in spring 1943 and some 2,600 were moved there, including Sinti from Vienna.

In Austria we hear of the first of the sadly few 'righteous Gorgios' — non-Gypsies who risked their lives to save Gypsies. Baron Rochunozy was determined that the Gypsies living on his land whose families had worked for him should not fall into the hands of the Nazis. He helped them to escape across the frontier into neighbouring Hungary, where they could conceal their identity and hopefully escape the later deportations from there. He himself then had to flee, narrowly escaping capture by the Nazi authorities.[29]

In February 1945 the Ministry of Justice sent a letter to the prison at Linz ordering that all Gypsies were to be shot when prisons near the front line were evacuated. The ultimate aim of Nazi policy in Austria was the death of the Austrian Gypsies. Less than a third were to survive. The more fortunate were those sent at an early stage to Lackenbach, who spent the war there in forced labour. Some communities were almost wiped out. Of the 275 Gypsies in Stegersbach, for example, only twenty-three survived.

Annexed lands

The Gypsies in other territories annexed to Greater Germany suffered fates similar to those in Austria. When Eupen, Malmedy and Moresner were joined to the Reich, Gypsies were specifically excluded from citizenship. The 1942 (2nd) Law on Citizenship in the new Eastern Territories, as they were called, made Gypsies there stateless.

Gypsies from the town of Tilsit were supposed to be sent to Lithuania in December 1941, unloaded there, and left to fend for themselves. But the authorities in Tilsit refused to do this. Instead, all of them — some 120, including children — were taken to Bialystok prison. In February of the following year orders came for the Gypsies living in the country around Tilsit to be sent to the camp in the Continerweg in Königsberg.

Edwin Klein was among those taken to Bialystok on 11 February 1942, and nine months later he was transferred to Brest-Litovsk camp. Marie Dombrowski also arrived in Brest-Litovsk from Bialystok in late 1942. The centre had been a camp for Russian prisoners of war; it was surrounded by barbed wire and the gate was locked at night. The men and some of the women worked in a concrete factory or on the railway but received no payment. In February 1943 the Jews in Brest-Litovsk were liquidated and the Gypsies put in their houses in the ghetto with a man from the Dombrowski family as head. No one was allowed to leave the ghetto and at least one person, Hermann Klein, was shot for this offence.

One group of Gypsies, the Flooki, worked on the land and were not rounded up. Nevertheless, some of the clan decided not to risk eventually sharing the fate of their fellow Gypsies and went to the forests. The men joined the partisans while their families remained in hiding.

East Prussia

East Prussia had been linked to Germany proper since 1939. In July 1941 the Security Central Headquarters ordered a settlement in Continerweg, Königsberg, to be turned into a guarded camp. Some 200 Gypsies, headed by another of the Dombrowski family, were interned there and lived under police surveillance. In the early days they could leave and enter the camp as they pleased.

The order to send East Prussian Gypsies to Auschwitz was made on 6 July 1942. A few were sent but not until April 1944 was the first large transport of some 850 male and female Gypsies dispatched. Gypsies from East Prussia were among those in the Organisation Todt labour camp at Valogne near Cherbourg in April 1944. Some were aged over sixty, all had been sterilised and they were put to work removing unexploded bombs.

Danzig

German troops marched into Danzig on 1 September 1939 and immediately began to beat up and kill Jews and Gypsies. During the first month a group of nomads was halted by German soldiers near the village of Czysta Woda, the next day being taken to the Jewish cemetery at Skarszewy and shot.

On 21 September it was agreed that Danzig Gypsies should be sent to Poland. Ten nomadic families were arrested and interned in an empty factory. Then, in October, together with families who had been living in houses, they were deported with their head man — named Wisanta — to an unknown destination, probably Stutthof concentration camp.[30]

THE CZECH LANDS — BOHEMIA AND MORAVIA

Under Nazi rule Czechoslovakia ceased to exist. The fate of the Gypsies varied considerably in the different parts into which the country was divided. We deal here with the Czech lands, Bohemia and Moravia, which were invaded and became a German protectorate in early 1939, before the official start of the Second World War. Slovakia and the Hungarian-occupied area are covered in a later chapter.

In March 1939 a special order was issued restricting nomadism and this was reinforced in November. That year two work-camps were opened and some nomadic families were sent to these. In 1942 a decree was issued under which the Gypsies' movements were to be controlled until such time as they could be deported to concentration camps.

Decree on the Fight against Crime

The following are the main provisions of this decree, which was modelled on the earlier German decree:

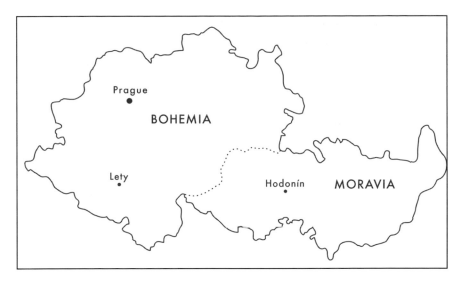

FIGURE 9. Map of the German protectorate of Bohemia and Moravia showing the concentration camps at Lety and Hodonín

In order to protect the community from all harmful persons, protective custody is herewith introduced. The persons to be placed into custody are . . . anyone who, without being a professional or habitual criminal, endangers the public through his asocial behaviour, beggars, Gypsies and persons travelling as Gypsies, prostitutes, persons with infectious diseases who do not follow the regulations of the Health Police . . . and work-shy persons.

Persons in protective custody will be held (a) in concentration camps in Bohemia and Moravia. (b) In the event of the concentration camps in the Protectorate proving insufficient, camps will be made available in Germany by the German Criminal Police. Hard labour camps will be turned into concentration camps . . . The Police Headquarters in Prague or the Police authorities in Brno will decide in which camp the person in protective custody is to be held.

There were special regulations for Gypsies:

Gypsies are forbidden to leave their place of residence without previous permission from Police Headquarters.

The distribution of licences to travel is to be transferred to the Criminal Police Headquarters. The previous agreement of the Criminal Police

Headquarters is necessary before permits or licences are issued for Gypsies to carry on nomadic trades.

All Gypsies had to register on 2 August 1942 and soon afterwards the Nazis began their removal to concentration camps.

Concentration camps

The two work camps which had been set up at Lety in southern Bohemia and Hodonín nad Kunstatem, in southern Moravia, were turned into concentration camps. About fifty Gypsies were also imprisoned in a work-camp in Dolni Markovice (Moravia) and another group in Osoblaze u Krnova, although these camps were not specifically intended for Gypsies.

As the two main camps soon became full, Gypsies were deported to camps outside the boundary of Bohemia and Moravia. Some were sent to Auschwitz well before the setting-up of the special Gypsy camp. They formed part of a mixed group from Brno that arrived there in April 1942 and also part of another mixed group comprising about sixty men and thirty-seven women, sent in December of the same year. Included in the latter transport was Ignancy Mrnka, no. 80735, who was shot after an unsuccessful attempt to escape in January 1943.[31]

Lety

According to the official records, over 1,200 Gypsies passed through the wooden barracks at Lety. In May 1943 the camp was closed and the prisoners were transferred, mainly to Auschwitz.

Conditions in the camp were poor and 327 of the registered prisoners died there. At first they were buried in the neighbouring town and then in a forest cemetery. Recently discovered evidence suggests that apart from those who died of disease a number of others were deliberately killed without being entered in the camp records. A survivor says that recaptured escapers were executed and that the first Camp Commander, Josef Janovsky, ordered the murder of pregnant women.

Hodonín

Hodonín camp at first held 300 persons before, in July 1942, three huts and a building were erected to bring the number to 800. Again, over 1,200 are noted in the camp records and, again, poor conditions took their toll. A total

FIGURE 10. Lety camp, Czechoslovakia

of 194 corpses was buried in a Catholic cemetery and in a mass grave oppo-
site the camp. After transports to Auschwitz and other concentration camps,
Hodonín was closed late in 1943.

Deportations

After the establishment of the special Gypsy Camp at Auschwitz, deportations increased. Between 11 March and 22 August 1943 over 3,000 were
transported there. Gypsies from Bohemia and Moravia comprised the second
largest national group in the camp, numbering over 4,000. Gypsies from the
Czech lands could also be found at Gross-Rosen and other camps.

Survivors

Few of the Gypsies in the Czech lands were to survive. Anna S. was born in
1943 at Pankrac prison in Prague. Straight after giving birth her mother was
killed but Anna was removed from the prison in a sack. Jan Daniel, from Moravia, survived, although injected with typhus and malaria at Natzweiler camp.[32]

Barbara Richter, Auschwitz no. Z.1963, born in 1929, has told her story,
from which we give two extracts:

At the beginning of the war my family were in Bohemia. My father had sold his caravan and taken a house. The Czech police came and took us to Lety. There were eighteen to twenty families there, all Gypsies. We were kept in barracks and not allowed to go out. This was in March or April 1941. In May I escaped. When I arrived in Prague a ticket-inspector gave me clothes and a hat to hide the fact that my hair had been shaved off.

She set off to escape across the border to Slovakia but returned to Prague and hid with a Gypsy family. Here she was betrayed by a police informer.

I was kept six weeks at the police station and then sent to Auschwitz [arriving there on 11 March 1943]. Later my family was released from Lety because the Richters were a well-established family in Bohemia. My mother came to Auschwitz voluntarily. Once I was given twenty-five blows with a whip because I had given some bread to a new arrival. One day I saw Elisabeth Koch kill four Gypsy children because they had eaten the remains of some food. Another time we stood for two hours in front of the crematorium but at the last moment were sent back to the barracks. I was given lashes a second time for taking bread from a dead prisoner. Three times they took blood from me. Dr Mengele injected me with malaria. I was then in the sick bay with my uncle. Some Gypsies carried me to another block just before all the patients in the sick bay, including my uncle, were killed.

Barbara and her mother were taken to Ravensbrück, probably on 15 April 1944. Six weeks later she was sent to a camp in Austria from which she escaped, making her way to Prague. There she was hidden by a Romany whom she later married. Her mother survived at Ravensbrück until the liberation.[33]

The official total of Gypsies in Bohemia and Moravia according to the information recorded on the registration day was just under 6,000. A few escaped to Slovakia. Of the rest nearly all eventually went to concentration camps in Germany and Poland and only 600 returned.

Occupation of western Europe

After annexing Austria and conquering Czechoslovakia the Germans then attacked Poland. This was the last straw for Britain and other countries in western Europe, who declared war on Germany in September 1939. The German army moved west and by 1940 had occupied Belgium, Denmark,

France, Holland, Luxembourg and Norway. All except France were placed under direct rule from Berlin. France was divided, as we describe below.

BELGIUM

The number of Gypsies living in Belgium was low. For about twenty families Belgium was their main country of residence, while others had been trapped there by the outbreak of the war. Many fled to France as the Germans invaded and were interned there, although some of those with Belgian nationality were later sent back to a transit camp in Malines.

In December 1941 the nomads were given a new identity document called, in Flemish, a *zigeunerkaart* (Gypsy card) which had to be stamped by the police on the fifth of each month. From January 1942 nomads were to be stopped on the road and allocated a fixed place to park. They were, however, left in comparative freedom until 1943.

Exceptionally, nine men were arrested early in 1943 by the German police for no apparent reason at the camp in Antwerp and lodged in the prison. They were eventually sent to the Gypsy Camp at Auschwitz in November 1943 with two other men and registered with the numbers Z.8887–8897. Of these, seven died in Auschwitz, two were transferred to Flossenburg, and one to Buchenwald, while there is no record of the fate of the remaining man (Ernest Vadoche) in the camp records.

From October 1943, on the orders of Himmler, all the nomadic Gypsies were to be arrested in Belgium and the part of northern France which was under the Nazi commander in Brussels. German police surrounded the encampments early in the morning and arrested everyone. A baby born in Brussels on 6 December was locked up on the same day with her mother in Dossin barracks at Malines (Mechelen). The other arrested Gypsies were gradually transferred to Malines, where they remained in poor conditions while the authorities assembled a larger transport. The 300 or more detainees were locked in three rooms with no toilets. They were let out each day to march around a courtyard for two hours, watched by guards with machine guns and accompanied by three violinists whose instruments were confiscated at the end of the 'recreation period'.

The detainees included 180 Gypsies of Belgian nationality or birth and 171 who possessed other nationalities or were stateless. An extract from the list of the eventual transport shows the range of birthplaces:

Charles and Waldemar Modis	Norway
Line Russalino	Stockholm
Jean Tchereanen	Oslo
P. Taicon	Barcelona
A. Reinhardt	Switzerland
A. Grunholz	Haarlem

When the transport finally left on 15 January 1944, the 351 Gypsies were loaded into cattle trucks with one piece of bread each for the three-day journey to Auschwitz.

At least forty of the prisoners listed on this transport were later transferred from Auschwitz to other camps. The rest died of disease or at the final liquidation of Auschwitz Gypsy Camp. Marie Maitre was one of the few survivors. Born in 1901 at Dixmuiden, Belgium, she had at the beginning of the war been in France and was interned first at Linas-Monthléry (Seine et Loire) and then at Montreuil. Later, classified as a Belgian, she was transferred to Malines. From Auschwitz she was taken to Ravensbrück and Buchenwald and, as the war ended, was repatriated to Belgium in May 1945.

Of the forty or so transported from Auschwitz only thirteen survived hard labour in the other camps and the final evacuations on foot to the west as the Soviet army advanced.

DENMARK

In neighbouring Denmark the sociologists Erik Bartels and Gudrun Brun published a study in which they argued that the Danish Travellers, in their opinion, were of Danish or German, not Romany, origin.[34] This study was published — surprisingly, in English — during the German occupation. It is not clear whether the German occupying forces had knowledge of this investigation but in the event no action was taken against the Travellers.

FRANCE

The French government had brought in severe restrictions against the movements of nomads after the outbreak of war but months before the German occupation. The authorities denied them the right to travel and placed them under police surveillance. Instructions to this effect, circulated to regional authorities on 6 April 1940, were published in the *Journal Officiel* three days later.

French rural police received a directive to stop Gypsies on the road and order them to move their caravans to a designated place. The task was made easier by the fact that since 1912 travelling Gypsies had been required to carry special identity cards marked *nomade* and were obliged by law to report to the police in each district.

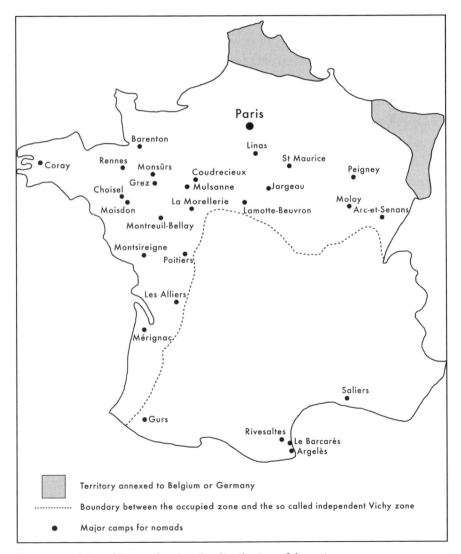

FIGURE 11. Map of France showing the distribution of the main camps

Once they had moved to the designated sites, Gypsies found their freedom restricted. They were allowed to go out to seek work but only in the district where they were camped. The police checked daily to see that the caravans had not moved.

Alsace

France capitulated to Germany in 1940. Alsace and the Moselle district were occupied and later annexed to Greater Germany. The German administration in Alsace, through several circulars, ordered the registration of Gypsies for the purpose of later deportation and to check that none returned to the province. This formed part of racial purification plans in preparation for the incorporation of the two provinces into the Reich. One such circular, headed 'Clearing Alsace of Gypsies', stated:

> It is intended to expel the Gypsies. They are to be put in a security camp at Schirmeck. During the operation Gypsies are to be kept separate from asocials and criminals. Non-Gypsy nomads are to be classed as Gypsies.

According to official correspondence, removal of the remaining Gypsies from Alsace took place before Christmas 1940. We know that in December the Germans deported a group of 146 'asocial' men and 403 women and children to France proper. Three weeks afterwards a list of evacuated Gypsies was sent to headquarters. However, this does not end the story. A year later another letter complains that the lists are not complete and that the Gypsies are proving a great burden on the community. As for the Moselle district, the Criminal Police decided in 1942 that they would not accept Gypsies from the area into Germany itself. Orders were that Gypsy groups were to be broken up, fortune-tellers arrested and those without work treated as asocials.

The Gypsies expelled from Alsace were to end up in a number of French internment camps. Twenty-five nomads expelled from the Moselle district arrived at Arc-et-Senans camp, after a two-day journey without food.

France divided

The northernmost districts of France came under the control of the Military Commander in Belgium and most Gypsies were expelled from there as well as from various border and coastal regions. A small area in the south-east was occupied by Italian troops while, until 1942, a zone in the south — the Vichy zone administered by the collaborator Marshal Pétain — kept some independence.

Internment

After the capitulation, a number of internment camps were set up at the request of the German authorities, but using the earlier French decree of 1940. The nomads were collected from their previously fixed places of residence and assembled in these camps. Reports which have recently become available show that they held around 3,000 Gypsy internees, a lower figure than was earlier thought. Supervision rested with the Ministry of the Interior, while French police and military personnel continued to make arrests and guarded the camps in both zones.

For a lengthy time the Germans and the French collaborators exploited Gypsies in all the camps for labour. No one knows the exact number who died as a result of the poor conditions. Official circles in France are still reticent about the subject because of French involvement. The fact that over thirty camps were under direct French administration has also been cloaked as far as possible and often denied.

The camps provided workers for farmers and industrial enterprises. Some centres had their own workshops for manufacturing and repairing various articles. They were not concentration camps, as no one was deliberately killed, but poor food and bad, overcrowded accommodation caused the mortality rate to soar, particularly among children. Conditions deteriorated as the war became prolonged. When conditions in a particular camp became unhygienic it was simply closed and the inmates moved by the authorities to other camps. This meant the breakdown of relationships with local employers and non-Gypsy contacts.

Discussion of selected camps

Montreuil

The internment camp at Montreuil (in the department of Maine-et-Loire) held 258 prisoners in November 1941. A medical examination by the Deputy Prefect of Saumur during the early days showed adults and children in poor physical condition. His report says: 'The children below the age of three are very thin, the pregnant women very anaemic . . . There is little wood available for heating.' During one nine-month period sixty-seven people died, mainly because of malnutrition.

The month after the camp opened, the Prefect of Finistère received instructions to send all nomads of 'Romany' type there. One party of 212 dispatched by him arrived without any luggage or even winter clothes. Internees arrived at Montreuil from other camps, including nearly 300 from La Morellerie. Other large groups came under escort from Mulsanne and Barenton. The camp population had risen to 1,043 by October 1942 but by December of the following year the number there had been reduced to 442 as a result of escapes and selective release of internees to fixed addresses.

Despite the armed guard at Montreuil, on the night of 11 December 1942, five men escaped. From then on visitors were prohibited, roll-calls held twice a day, money confiscated and patrols strengthened. A few fortunate inmates were permitted, on condition that they remained at fixed places of work under police surveillance, to live away from the camp at a distance of twenty kilometres or more from the centre of the town.

During Allied air-raids in 1944 bombs fell several times on Montreuil, damaging buildings. On New Year's Day the following year the camp was

FIGURE 12. Camp at Montreuil-Bellay

broken up. The remaining inmates were sent to Jargeau and Les Alliers and some — those who had homes to go to — were actually released.

Mulsanne

Gypsies collected from smaller camps at Coudrecieux, Linas-Monthléry and Moisdon la Rivière were gathered together at Mulsanne — a former British army camp in the department of Sarthe — and numbered 700 soon after the opening in April 1942. The daily vegetable ration at Mulsanne amounted to 400g of potatoes or 500g of other vegetables, sometimes replaced by 100g of dry vegetables. The meat ration hardly averaged 126g per week. The prisoners lived in their family groups and 100 men worked in the Renault motor factory at Le Mans. Taken daily to work by lorry, a few managed to escape, helped by the fact that the guards were not always fully armed. The camp was closed late in 1942 and the internees transported to Montreuil.

Poitiers

The Poitiers camp in Viennes department operated from 1940 to 1944. It stood a few miles from the town on the Limoges road. The barracks there had previously housed refugees from the Spanish Civil War, as had the camp at Gurs in the Vichy zone. A double barbed-wire fence and four watch-towers with searchlights hemmed in the Gypsy occupants at Poitiers, who were cordoned off from the Jews and women political prisoners in other compounds. The French administration permitted some visitors, and one who came regularly for a period from February 1942 onwards was Madame G. L'Huillier. Selflessly concerned about the families' plight, she eventually received permission to give lessons to the children. On occasion she was even allowed to take them for walks outside the wire perimeter. She recalled there would have been serious trouble had any tried to escape while enjoying this privilege. Later a small building was erected for the classes. A Catholic priest, Father J. Fleury, conducted a service there in May 1942 and noted that the guards seldom ventured inside the prisoners' huts for fear of disease.

At the end of 1943 there was a large transport from Poitiers to Montreuil. Father J. Fleury followed the internees to Montreuil, as did Madame L'Huillier. Another cleric, Abbé Jollec, also helped the internees after their arrival at Montreuil. The camp at Poitiers was finally closed in 1944 and the remaining detainees also moved to Montreuil.

Detention outside the camps

A very limited number of Gypsies at Barenton camp (La Manche depart-ment) secured conditional release on being assigned to particular work with local employers. They remained in barrack-type accommodation under the control of the police. Paul Weiss was among those imprisoned at St Jean Pied de Port for leaving his allotted place of work under a similar scheme.

Jose Santiago, arrested and placed in a forced labour squad in the old fort at Romainville (on the outskirts of Paris), escaped and went to Amiens. Caught again by the French police, he was asked why he was not doing com-pulsory work. He gave a story which somehow persuaded them to release him and made his way to the Vichy zone, remaining there undetected.

Deportations

In 1943 the German authorities introduced compulsory work service (*Serv-ice du Travail Obligatoire*) in Germany for young Frenchmen. In January and again in June 1943 a group of Gypsy men was taken from Poitiers camp and sent to Compiègne. Here they were given a physical examination. Eighty-nine of these men were sent to Germany, in theory to work in factories, although in practice they ended up in the concentration camps of Sachsen-hausen and Buchenwald. Michael Weiss, then aged thirteen, was taken from Compiègne to Block 31 in the main camp at Buchenwald, while two adults from his family found themselves in the Dora satellite camp.

Other Gypsies volunteered to go and work in Germany, thinking life would be better than in the camps. Among them was Frans Josef. He soon realised his mistake, got a doctor to certify him as unfit for work and was returned to France. On the way he escaped. Arrested again, he tried to flee a second time and this time succeeded, although he was shot in the arm. After the war he made his way to Norway.

The Vichy zone

The puppet Vichy government initially used three camps which had been built for refugees from the Spanish Civil War (Argelès, Barcarès and Rivesal-tes — all in the Pyrenées Orientales department). These were mainly used for nomads expelled from Alsace. In 1942 the Vichy government set up a new camp at Saliers (in Bouche du Rhone), built initially by nomads from the Barcarès camp. It was intended to be a model camp as well as financially self-supporting, thanks to basket-working.

Other internment camps held some Gypsies. Ten children from a mixed camp at Noé were successfully smuggled across the border into Switzerland.

Beyond the camps

Nomadic Gypsies in northern France, which was administered from Brussels, were arrested and sent to Malines camp in Belgium. Among these were the Schmitt family, arrested in 1943 in Roubaix and sent in 1944 to Malines and then to Auschwitz. Gypsies with Belgian nationality were transferred from camps in France proper to Malines and followed the same path thereafter.

Another family caught by German soldiers (probably a detachment of Das Reich division) were massacred at the roadside in the department of Lot-et-Garonne during 1944. We shall see later that the ordinary units of the German army took part in many massacres of Gypsies in the occupied countries of the east. Paul Wanderstein, then aged twelve, survived to recount what happened in this incident:

> It was early morning about dawn at the entrance to the village of Saint Sixte when the soldiers found us. They took fourteen of us into a field to be shot. My mother, two sisters — the younger four years old, the elder Anne, aged nine — my grandmother, an uncle and cousins were among those lined up. Two of them and one of my girl cousins lay only wounded but appeared dead. Three others escaped by running into the village and hiding in the school loft. I don't remember exactly what happened but I was concealed somehow in the village and saved.

Surprisingly, in 1942, despite the troubled times, the annual Gypsy festival at Les Saintes Maries in the Camargue (held each year towards the end of May) went ahead. Although attended by Gypsies from Spain, it was a subdued gathering that year, overshadowed by menaces. The remoteness of the region, set with reed-filled lagoons, and the presence of Italian officials in the neighbouring Italian-occupied area, militated against a ban — or, worse still, a round-up. In the following year the festival was suppressed by the Vichy authorities.

Those who realised in time what the fall of France would bring had a slender chance to get out of the country. Gypsies in the south with relations in Spain and North Africa could slip over the border into Spanish territory. But although the Franco regime paid little attention to them once in Spain, the way over the Pyrenees was restricted. From northern France a handful reached England.

House-dwelling Gypsy men and youths — previously untroubled by the Germans — were rounded up for the first time from 1943 alongside other young Frenchmen to join the thousands doing forced labour in Germany. There are no accurate figures for the number of Gypsies deported or for the number who died in the harsh conditions.

One man, Louis Simon, born at Périgueux, met a particularly bizarre death. It was noticed that his body was richly tattooed — a souvenir from service in the Foreign Legion. First he was given injections which caused him to swell horribly and die, following which his dead body was carried to Buchenwald and the skin used as a decoration for a shelf.

The resistance

Some Gypsies who stayed free outside the camps joined the resistance. Jean Beaumarie helped the Maquis, as did his brother, who was caught and hanged. Armand Stenegry, later President of the Manouche Gypsy Association and well known as a singer and guitarist under the name Archange, became a guerrilla officer. Stenegry and other Gypsies in his unit assisted in partisan attacks planned to coincide with the Normandy landings. His distinguished service earnt him decoration both by the British and the Free French. Henri Roussin, a basket-maker, joined the French resistance at the age of seventeen. He was caught and deported to Buchenwald where he was held until 1945.

The invasion of France by Allied troops in 1944 may be the reason why deportations from the camps to Germany stopped. The end of the war did not, however, bring freedom for all the internees. The French team for the Inspection of Administrative Services said in September 1945 that it was 'not opportune' to release the nomads, and inmates at Jargeau (in Loiret) were not released until 31 December 1945.

Algeria

Finally, we must add that in Algeria, which had been governed by France, Gypsies did not escape persecution. Although the wealthier passed as Spanish and escaped attention, poorer Gypsies were pushed together into a ghetto at Maison-Carre near Algiers. The quarter held about 700 and some died there. Others were rounded up at Oran and Mostaganem.

HOLLAND (THE NETHERLANDS)

The Nazi-controlled press began a campaign of propaganda against Gypsies in June 1942. *Nord Brabantsche Courant* reported a 'plague' of Gypsies in the provinces of Brabant and Limburg. It was said that the nuisance they caused had increased enormously and that a central caravan camp should be established under police supervision.

Johan Grunholz was arrested in The Hague in 1942 and was sent to a forced labour camp in Amersfoort. He escaped on the journey there and went to Eindhoven to warn relatives that Gypsies were being arrested, only to find they had disappeared. Arrested in Eindhoven, he was taken back to Amersfoort. The prisoners there were given numbers, their hair was shaved and they had to wear striped clothing. From Amersfoort he was sent to Buchenwald.

In May 1943 the head of the SS in Holland, Hanns Rauter, banned nomadism. Horses were to be taken away and twenty-seven camps, to hold some 1,200 caravans, were set up for Gypsies and other caravan-dwellers.

A few Gypsies, as well as some of the local Dutch travelling population, known as *woonwagenbewoners*, sold their caravans and moved into houses rather than go into the camps. This did not save them all. We know that when the time came for the Dutch Gypsies from the camps to be sent to Auschwitz Theresia Wagner was arrested by Dutch police in a house in The Hague and then transported to the concentration camp.

To Auschwitz

Himmler had ordered the deportation of the Dutch Gypsies to Auschwitz as early as March 1943, although the actual deportation did not take place until the following year. The arrests were planned in secret and the Gypsies had no warning. On 14 May 1944 the regional police chiefs were ordered to pick up all persons with the 'characteristics of Gypsies'. Early in the morning two days later Gypsies and a number of Dutch caravan-dwellers were picked up from the camps and elsewhere in a special sweep and taken to Westerbork. Here they had their heads shaved and their money and jewels taken away.

Tatta Hanstein's family were the only ethnic Gypsies on the caravan site in Helmond. They had just gone to bed at 1 A.M., having celebrated Tatta's father's birthday in a cafe that evening. An hour later there was banging on the door: 'Open up. If you don't open, we shoot.'

They were Dutch SS men. Tatta and his family were marched to the police station. On the way, one brother managed to slip away into the woods. By 6 A.M. the others had already been sent on their way to Westerbork. At Westerbork a selection was made on racial grounds and a few of the prisoners were released. Then a transport of 245 persons was sent to Auschwitz, arriving on 21 May.

Tatta Hanstein was later moved from Auschwitz to Buchenwald and Harzung. He escaped, but was recaptured and sentenced to seventy-five strokes. He collapsed after fifty. When he recovered, the remaining twenty-five were meted out. He was then returned to Buchenwald and — as were many other Gypsies — sent on to Bergen-Belsen where he was released by Allied troops in May 1945. He lost his father, mother, eight brothers and two sisters.

This deportation reduced the surviving Gypsies in Holland to a handful. Some were probably later sent to the camp for 'asocials' at Ommen and from there to work-camps and factories in Germany. One extended family who did escape the net were the Baba Tshurkeshti who held Nicaraguan passports. They were interned in Holland for the duration of the war.

Sixteen-year-old Edi Georg was not picked up because he was sleeping with his horses in a stable in order to keep them safe. The rest of his family were arrested in their caravans and taken to Westerbork and Auschwitz. A Dutchman, Hendrik Bethlehem, helped Edi to get a false identity and a place to hide until the end of the war. Inspector Knol of the Dutch police saved the lives of four families by telling the Germans that they were Dutch musicians, while Tata Mirando and his family were freed from a cell in Doetinchem by a German officer whose violin he had repaired.

Of the 245 Gypsies sent to Auschwitz, it is believed that 145 died or were killed there. Of the 100 later sent on from Auschwitz to other camps, only thirty survived.

LUXEMBOURG

Gypsies in Luxembourg were covered by Himmler's Auschwitz order. Although no contemporary records survive, their presence in the camp was mentioned at the war crimes trial of Eichmann in Jerusalem.[35]

NORWAY

At the time of the German conquest in 1940 there was no one who would have been racially classed as a Romany Gypsy in the country. However, there were several thousand Travellers known as *tatere* or *omstreifere*, many of whom were certainly of part-Romany descent. The move for action against these Travellers seems to have been initiated by an official in the Social Welfare Department of Oslo borough. He wrote to the Chief of the Security Police on 3 March 1943 suggesting that the Travellers should be interned and then removed from the country; that same month he published an article in the paper *Fritt Folk* saying that the problem of Travellers must be solved.

Although there is no record of a reply to the official, the Chief of the Security Police wrote to Minister Jonas Lie, who replied at the end of March, saying:

> The simplest solution is of course, as suggested by the Chief of Police, to collect together all the Gypsies and Travellers [*tatere och omstreifere*] and export them to Poland.

The Prime Minister Vidkon Quisling wrote in June to the Minister of Justice:

> On my travels I see that there are still bands of Gypsies on the roads. There is good reason to take up the Traveller problem in the broadest sense, that is from a racial hygiene viewpoint.

At the end of June a proposal to register all Travellers was circulating among ministers. The official in the Social Welfare Department was still pursuing the matter and wrote to Lie proposing an internment camp. By July the Prime Minister had agreed with Lie's proposal to set up a special work camp under guard, and to put in it all Travellers with Gypsy blood. Their horses and boats would be taken away and there would be a racial investigation of the Travellers and sterilisation of Gypsies 'with criminal genes':

> First of all [wrote Lie] the campaign will be against criminals but the aim is to get a final solution of the Gypsy plague in the way the Jewish question had been resolved, that is by deportation to the concentration camps.

Oscar Lyngstad, General Secretary of the Norwegian Mission for the Homeless, offered the Mission's card index of Travellers to the Police Department. The plan for a work camp was not pursued, and, after some delay, a working party was set up with representatives of the Police Department, the Ministry of the Interior and the Social Welfare Department. The first meeting was on 3 November 1944 and they managed to fit in fourteen meetings before 22 December. The working party decided that the matter should be handled by first of all stopping nomadism and then by sexual intervention (i.e. sterilisation) to stop the Travellers breeding.

A draft law was drawn up. Anyone who had travelled in Gypsy fashion during the last five years would have to report to the police and give information about themselves. Such persons could not own a horse, boat or car. Any nomadising would have to be on foot. An amendment was proposed to an earlier law on Preserving the National Heritage: anyone who was found wandering around in Gypsy fashion would be investigated with a view to sterilisation or castration. The last reference to the Traveller question in government minutes is dated 10 March 1945. On 7 May Germany capitulated to the Allies before any of the proposed measures could take effect.

EUROPE UNDER THE NAZIS:

OCCUPIED COUNTRIES IN THE EAST

POLAND

On 1 September 1939, German troops invaded Poland. Later in the month Soviet troops entered the country from the east and on 29 September Poland was partitioned, not for the first time in its history.

For the Nazis Poland was a convenient place to dump Germany's unwanted Jews and Gypsies, and some 3,000 of the latter were sent there during 1940. The administrative machinery in Poland seems to have been unprepared for the large deportations into western Poland of Jews and Gypsies from Germany; no real provision was made for the Gypsies who arrived in 1940 and some of them ended up living in the towns alongside Polish Gypsies.

In June 1941 Germany attacked the Soviet Union and soon occupied the rest of Poland. Persecution of the Gypsies then began in earnest, the declared policy being to put the Gypsies in ghettos and work-camps.

In the ghettos

In May 1942, Gypsies living anywhere in the Warsaw region were instructed to go to the nearest Jewish ghetto. If they then moved away they would be fined or sent to prison. In June that year all Gypsies in the Ostrow–Masowiecki region were moved to the ghettos. Ghettos with Gypsy sections included Belapodlaska, Chelm, Cracow, Kielce, Kostopol, Lublin, Praga (in Warsaw), Radom, Sanck, Siedlce, Tschenstochau and Wengrow. Conditions varied from comparative freedom in some to concentration-camp conditions in others. Usually the Gypsies had to wear a white armband with a blue Z on it. There were also labour camps in Rabka-Zaryte and Warsaw-Marimont. At labour camps run by the army in Postkow, Szebnie and Zastaw at least 117 Gypsies were shot at the whim of the commanding officers.

One survivor has recounted how his uncle was shot in Warsaw in front of the whole family for buying trousers from a Russian. On another occasion he himself was put in front of a wall with ten other Gypsy children and some Jews to be shot. At the last moment an SS officer came and took the Gypsies away.[36]

The authorities tried to work up public opinion against the Gypsies, and towards the end of 1942 the *Krakower Zeitung* and the *Lemberger Zeitung* broke out with a rash of articles whose thrust was that it was intolerable to let an entire race of parasites go on eating while Europe was suffering hunger as a result of the Allied blockade. Despite this, the Gypsies in Lemberg, while they were kept in the ghetto, were allowed to go in and out freely and practise their traditional trades until 1944.

FIGURE 13. German soldier shooting a victim

Massacres

From 1942 large-scale massacres of Gypsies, often by Polish and Ukrainian fascists, took place in many parts of Poland, while other groups were sent to concentration and extermination camps.

In all, 115 Gypsies were killed at Lohaczy in 1942, as were 96 at Szczurowa and 15 at Berna in 1943; 104 were killed at Zahcroczyma, about 50 at Karczew and 30 at Grochow. In Olyce all the Gypsies were shot, and other murders took place at Komorow, Pyrach, Radom, Sluzeca, Targowka and Zyradow. Dogs were let loose on the Gypsies of Poznan. Mass executions took place in Wolyn (Wolhynia) and the Carpathians. In Wolyn province about 3,000 to 4,000 Gypsies died at the hands of German and Ukrainian fascists. Only the adults were shot. The children were often murdered by being seized by the legs and having their heads smashed against tree trunks. Mobile gas chambers were also used. Another group was drowned when they were driven on to a river covered with thin ice. One report said that the Ukrainian fascists spared the local Ukrainian Gypsies and killed only those who were Polish.

The killings continued. In May 1944 twenty-eight nomadic Gypsies were arrested near Lipiny (Bilgoraj). The German police found out they were musicians and made them play for four days and nights, before forcing them to strip and taking them to a graveyard where they — including a new-born baby — were killed. The children, again, were murdered by being swung against trees. The adults were shot and buried, alive or dead.

In addition to the many hundreds killed indiscriminately, including in the ghettos themselves, Gypsies faced transportation to Auschwitz, Belsen, Chelmno, Maidenek and Treblinka. About 600 Polish Gypsies, as well as 2,600 from Bialystok, are known to have been sent to Auschwitz. It is estimated that at least 8,000 persons (a quarter of the Polish Gypsies) lost their lives during the Nazi occupation. This is in addition to those brought from other countries and killed in the death camps in Poland.

Rudolf Kwiek

In Poland the German authorities had some dealings with a representative of the Gypsies (as they did with those of the Jews). Although Janusz I Kwiek, who had been elected King of the Polish Gypsies, was arrested early in the war, there was some contact between the German occupiers and Rudolf Kwiek, his rival. In a letter written as early as 1941 he apparently offered to point out the hiding places of Polish Gypsies in exchange for safe-conduct passes for sixteen members of his family, expressing his wish to be of service to the German cause. In 1947 he was put on trial as a collaborator. Witnesses testified that Kwiek had arrived in a Gypsy settlement with the Gestapo before the inhabitants were taken off to be executed. Other witnesses, however, supported Kwiek, and he was found not guilty. The letter mentioned above was not found until after his death in 1964.[37]

Survivors

Few of the Polish Gypsies who were deported to Auschwitz survived. Hanna Brzezinska was a teenager when the Germans came to her village; all the men there, including her father, were shot after being made to dig their own graves. The women and children were driven into lorries and taken to Auschwitz. Her number was Z.4517. One day she was taken with some other Gypsies to clean an empty Jewish camp. When she returned to Auschwitz she found all the remaining members of her family had disappeared. Then taken to Ravensbrück, she worked making rings, but after a while was transferred to Rechlin and then to Maidenek. She was chosen for the gas chamber and tied up with a Jewish girl for twenty-four hours while awaiting her turn. Spared at the last minute, she was moved to a munitions factory at Hamburg where there were some other Gypsies. She stayed there until the end of the war.[38]

Another survivor recounted how he escaped a massacre:

> They put us behind barbed wire and imprisoned us at Jadowa. Then all the men were collected and locked in the synagogue. I was still small, a child, so they let me stay with the women. Later they hauled the men out of the synagogue and shot them all. So in the night we cut the wires and escaped. From there we went to Darczew but there was no peace there either. Not long after, the Germans began to kill the Gypsies. There were two houses full of Gypsies. They threw small children out of high windows on to the cobble stones and there was a lot of blood. I hobbled to a restaurant where two of my brothers were drinking vodka. They hadn't yet heard what had happened to the Gypsies. I told them and we escaped. One brother had a revolver and when the Gestapo started to chase us, he shot two of them.[39]

YUGOSLAVIA

The Gypsy community in Yugoslavia was largely sedentary and numbered several hundred thousand. Events overtook them. The Prince Regent Paul signed a treaty with the Axis Powers (Germany and Italy), which came as a deadly blow, the first serious indication that the fate already befalling the Gypsies in Germany was likely to be visited on those in Yugoslavia as well. The young King Peter organised a coup against the Regent, as he and his advisers realised that the treaty with Germany would involve Yugoslavia in an attack on Greece, but this brought only a momentary reprieve.

A merciless bombing of Belgrade, which also hit the Gypsy quarter in Zemun, preceded the German invasion of Yugoslavia on 5 April 1941,

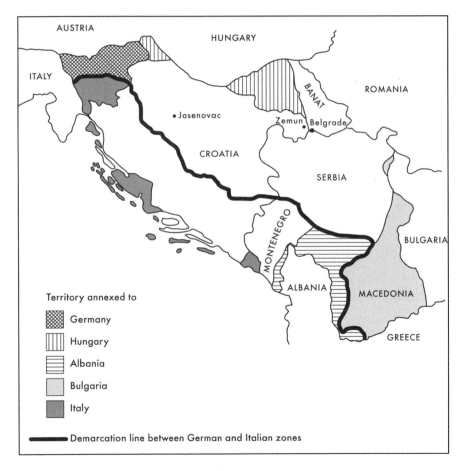

FIGURE 14. Map showing the division of Yugoslavia in 1941

and the blitzing of southern Greece. Thereafter the young state was to be torn to pieces and divided up between the invaders (Germans, Bulgarians, Hungarians and Italians), the collaborators in Croatia and their opponents, the Partisans.

In all areas uncoordinated guerrilla bands came into being to attack the occupation forces or simply to survive in the mountains, while protecting families fleeing from the towns and villages. The murders and wholesale extermination of Gypsies in Croatia and Serbia caused an increased number of Gypsies to join the National Liberation Front (NLF), which emerged as the most effective fighting organisation. Because of Gypsies' participation in the war effort, serious consideration was given within the NLF to the creation of an autonomous Gypsy region in Macedonia as part of the planned new Yugoslavia federation. This did not happen.

For the convenience of the reader we deal with Yugoslavia below in terms of the present-day geographical divisions: Kosovo, Macedonia, Serbia and Voivodina (with Banat), while the puppet state of Croatia is left to the next chapter. We give below also such little information as is known about events in Montenegro and Slovenia (occupied by the Italians).

KOSOVO

Kosovo, bordering on Albania, was garrisoned by pro-Axis Albanians — the Balisti — under Italian command, and there were also some German SS troops there. Local Albanians also joined the SS. Gypsies were made to wear armbands but remained free in the early years, although when Kosovo-born Albanians were recruited to the fascist armies Gypsies were forced to take their jobs. Some young Gypsies were even conscripted, as their identity was not known; several deserted, and were shot. After the capitulation of the Italians, the partisans succeeded in liberating the territory and many Gypsies then joined the Liberation Front.

An outline of events affecting the community in the town of Kosovska-Mitrovica was given by Kuna Cevcet:

> At this time there were three or four hundred Gypsy households in the town and we made up about a tenth of the population of Mitrovica. Those above the age of fifteen who had been identified had to wear a yellow arm-band about four inches wide with the word *Zigeuner* on it. We were not permitted to wear moustaches, which were very common.

It seems the fascists didn't want to see us wearing them.

On 16 May 1942, we gathered to celebrate a festival, and began killing sheep for the feast. But at half-past four in the morning SS troops, accompanied by Albanian police, came into the town and took away all the slaughtered sheep in lorries for their own use.

Ljatif Sucuri, an uncle of mine who was about thirty-five at this time, knew the Albanian chief of police, a general. When an order came through for the police to round up Gypsies Ljatif Sucuri told him that if any Gypsies were killed he would personally kill the police chief and the rest of us would burn down the houses of the Albanians. He told the police chief to inform his superiors over the telephone that there were no Gypsies at Mitrovica, and this he did.

Ljatif Sucuri went on with his efforts to save his people, using his influence with the Albanian police chief. The day the police chief came with a paper from higher authorities ordering him to kill all Gypsies, Ljatif Sucuri got him to hand over the paper — and then burnt it. Once again he got him to telephone his superiors and say there were no Gypsies in the town, only Muslims. This was about August or September 1943.

As a result of his intervention, no Gypsies were murdered in Mitrovica itself. Many people were hanged, however, for helping the partisans.

A resistance worker

At this time there were few Gypsies with the partisans because they feared that the fascists would kill their families. But later, when the partisans became stronger, they joined. However, one Gypsy in Mitrovica, Hasan Ibrahim, then aged thirty-six, was already in the resistance in 1943. He worked as a mechanic in a garage being run by the military for repairing vehicles and storing petrol, and would get petrol and make petrol bombs for the partisans.

After he had supplied bombs for a time, the partisans suggested that he should blow up the garage and stores. He set to work and, using more petrol bombs, succeeded in setting fire to the whole garage, destroying many military vehicles and petrol supplies and quantities of other stores. Subsequently, he was arrested and held in prison but as there was no proof against him he was released after a week and continued to work at the depot. He went on making petrol bombs and later set fire to the military food stores in the town. Then he helped to steal arms and passed them on to the partisans. In 1944

Ibrahim went to the mountains with the partisans and remained with them until the end of the war. He received many decorations in recognition of his service and went back to his old job in Mitrovica.

Forced labour

Meanwhile, those Gypsies who had been identified and wore armbands were selected to work for the military. They had to build barracks for the army and carry food supplies and munitions to the front.

About 200 or 300 were allocated to forced labour during 1942 and they started off from the town driving animals — cows and sheep — for the soldiers. The soldiers rode on horseback and continually beat the Gypsies to make them move faster. They had to travel hundreds of kilometres across the mountains and into Greece. This work went on for three or four months. Many Gypsies deserted and made contact with the partisans, and four whom the fascists believed assisted the partisans were arrested when they tried to desert. They were beaten to get information out of them and then hanged in public in a Greek town in front of the other Gypsies and the townspeople. Those hanged were Djemajl Maljoku, Jalil Avjija, Ramadan Dibrani and a fourth man called Bajram.

When Ljatif Sucuri heard about their deaths he again went to the police chief, demanding an explanation. This time he succeeded in persuading the chief to have the remaining Gypsies from Mitrovica released from the labour brigade, himself going to Greece to see that this was done.

At the end of the war collaborators, trying to cover up their own activities, denounced Ljatif Sucuri and said he had cooperated with the occupiers. Without checking the allegations, the partisans took him away in the night and shot him.

MACEDONIA

The whole of Macedonia, both Greek and Yugoslav, with the exception of the port of Salonika, came under Bulgarian occupation. Fortunately for the Gypsy population, the Bulgarians — with an enormous Gypsy community in their own country — felt disinclined to take severe measures, whatever Germany might want. The deportation of the Jews from Skopje in May 1943 sounded a warning, however. As time wore on, German security police became active in the region and some Gypsies fell into the net.

Several factors hindered the rooting-out, however, and enabled Gypsies, despite their great numbers, to avoid detection. Many owned land or worked as farm labourers and most nominally followed the Muslim religion. In the countryside they were indistinguishable from neighbouring Turks and Albanians of the same occupation and faith, at least as far as outsiders were concerned.

The situation was just as confusing in the towns. When a population census took place most Gypsies entered themselves under the heading of another minority. Not wanting to court trouble with Turks and Albanians, the police allowed false declarations to pass unchallenged, but if identity was obvious they closed in. A circus family, who had been performing in Turkey and Bulgaria, came to Skopje in 1943 and were arrested. Taken first to the camps in Crveni Krst and Zemun in Serbia, they finally ended up in Auschwitz.[40]

Others, their identity betrayed by people helping the occupation authorities, had to wear yellow armbands. Some were taken as forced labourers to Bulgaria.

MONTENEGRO

After the fall of Yugoslavia, Montenegro was occupied by Italian soldiers and the Gypsies were apparently left unharmed. However, when the Germans took over the occupation of Italian-held areas of Yugoslavia and Albania in the autumn of 1943, they had a year to impose their extreme policies against Gypsies, and during this period people are believed to have been sent to concentration camps in Yugoslavia, as well as to Buchenwald, Mauthausen and elsewhere.

SERBIA

In May 1941, five weeks after the occupation of Serbia, the military administration issued a series of decrees concerning the Gypsies. For example, neither a Gypsy nor anyone married to a Gypsy was allowed to run a theatre or cinema. Trams and buses bore placards saying 'No Jews or Gypsies allowed'. The German army commander General Franz Böhme sent out a further decree at the end of the month, which included the following provisions:

Section 18: Gypsies are to be treated as Jews.

Section 19: A Gypsy is someone with three Gypsy grandparents. Part-Gypsies who have at least one Gypsy grandparent and who are married to a Gypsy are also to be classed as Gypsies.

Section 20: Gypsies are to be put on a special register and wear yellow armbands inscribed with Z [for *Zigeuner*]

Men became liable to forced labour and mass arrests began. In the village of Jabuce (near Belgrade) and the surrounding area 250 Gypsies were arrested. Milan Milanović watched his father and two uncles being taken from their homes:

> My father had only time to say goodbye to our mother and us three children and then he was put into one of the lorries waiting in the street. We never saw him again.

Most of those arrested in the early months were not in fact sent for forced labour, but were held and eventually shot as 'hostages'.

A Romany who had risen to be a district judge, Jovan Jovanović, has described his position at this period:

> During the occupation, I had to tell everyone, even persons I knew well, that I wasn't a Gypsy and had no connections with Gypsies. If I hadn't lied I would have had to carry the outcast's label on my arm and who knows if I'd still be alive.
>
> Despite the orders, one day on leaving my judge's office I entered a restaurant. Instead of the waiter, the manager came in person to tell me in rough terms to get out because I was a Gypsy. I calmly showed him my papers. Seeing I was a judge he excused himself saying that he'd made a mistake because of the colour of my skin.[41]

Hostages

In October 1941 the Chief of Civil Administration in Serbia, Harald Turner, issued a memorandum to local German commanders:

> The Gypsy cannot, by reason of his inner and outer make-up, be a useful member of the society of nations . . . As a matter of principle it must be said that the Jews and Gypsies represent an element of insecurity and thus a danger to public order and safety . . . That is why it is a matter of principle in each case to put all Jewish men and all male Gypsies at the disposal of the troops as hostages.

For every German soldier shot by the partisans 100 hostages were to be executed. On 12 and 13 October that year Jews and Gypsies were killed as hostages by the soldiers of the 718th Division together with the 64th Reserve Police Battalion at Sabac (Zastavica), while on 17 October Turner wrote to a friend in Danzig: 'In the last eight days I had 2,000 Jews and 200 Gypsies shot in accordance with the ratio 1:100.'

On 29 October, to swell the pool of hostages, 250 Gypsies were arrested in Belgrade. On 22 December, because of a continuing shortage of hostages, General Paul Bader (who had replaced General Böhme as commander of the occupying army) reduced the reprisal ratio to 1:50. The hostages were to include Communists captured without weapons, Gypsies and Jews. Ordinary Serbs were to be spared because the Germans hoped to win over the civilian population.

The firing squads were composed of regular German army units. About the shootings a junior officer reported:

> One has to admit that the Jews are very composed when they go to their deaths — they stand still — while the Gypsies cry, scream and move constantly, even when they are already on the spot where they are to be shot. Some even jumped into the ditch before the firing and pretended to be dead.[42]

Regular troops mobilised for a punitive expedition shot down 250 Gypsies caught on the road and burnt their wagons. In another incident at Kragujevac soldiers rounded up 200 who happened to have come into the town and machine-gunned the men and boys on the local shooting range, alongside a larger number of Serbians, in reprisal for ten dead and twenty-six wounded Germans. Some Gypsy boys were made to clean the blood from the shoes of the German soldiers before they too, were shot. A German soldier who refused to take part in the murder was himself shot and buried in a separate grave.

Shooting of Gypsies as hostages was to continue in eastern Serbia and, because of the practice of selecting men as hostages, the occupying authorities found themselves with numerous bereaved women and children under their charge. The answer was to concentrate them at a camp in Sajmište.

The camps

The first camp for Gypsies in Serbia was at Sajmište, near Zemun, where an exhibition ground had been turned into a concentration camp for Jews. At one time it held 600 Gypsies in separate unheated halls, in which the inmates slept on straw.

Olga Milanović was one of those imprisoned. She remembers the poor food:

> I was only five years old when our family was arrested in Belgrade and taken to the camp at Zemun. My father died later, I believe in Germany. After our arrest I was in the camp for three months. They gave us rotten potatoes and water soup. The ration was one hundred grams a day.

A second camp at Topovska Shupa was more of a holding camp for Gypsies while a third, at Banjica, could be classed as an extermination camp. Many of the several thousand Gypsy and other prisoners who were taken there were shot on the first morning after their arrival.

The gas van

In 1942 Heinrich Müller (Chief of the Gestapo) offered a gas van to Emmanuel Schäfer (Director of Security in Belgrade) to kill the Jews in Sajmište. The same van was used for Gypsies there. Loaded regularly with women and children, the van was driven to the woods. There they were gassed and the bodies buried. Their possessions were passed to the German Welfare Agency, which transferred them to Germany itself for distribution among the German civilian population.

Niš

When the Germans first came to Niš in 1941 they had said that Gypsies could not leave their houses unless they wore a yellow armband bearing the word *Zigeuner*. The Germans went round the houses and shaved everyone's heads on the pretext that they had lice, but everyone was shaved whether they had lice or not. They arrested men from time to time and took them away. An eyewitness describes the raids:

> At night the Germans — Gestapo and others in civilian clothes — came to the house with one of the two Gypsy mayors. One of these collaborated with the Germans and the other did not. He tried to warn people that the Germans had come and shouted [in Romani]: 'Run away, Gypsies, they are coming again.' There would be a lorry outside the house with guards. Three or four men would come into the houses with the

mayor and sometimes they hit the men, sometimes they did not, and they lied, saying, 'You are going to work. Come along'.

The Gypsies from Niš were taken to a camp in Crveni Krst. Many Gypsies were then shot as hostages at a place called Mount Bubanj. One report speaks of 100 Gypsies shot on one day. A memorial has since been erected on the hill.

FIGURE 15. Niš concentration camp, Serbia

A survivor's story

Zekia A. was eight years old when the Germans occupied Niš. She lived with her family in Stočni, the Gypsy quarter. Left alone when her brothers, and soon afterwards her parents, were arrested by the Germans, she first stayed with some women whose menfolk had also been taken by the Nazis. One day in the market a Serb called Milan from a neighbouring village saw her. He knew her, as her parents had helped with the harvest on his farm. When he learnt that all her family had been arrested he took her to his village, Čamrlija. He and his wife Lepa dressed her in the clothes of a Serbian to look like a Serbian girl. As Germans came to the house daily to take hens and eggs, she had to spend the day in the fields looking after the sheep. Only at night did she dare return to the farm. The Germans also came to the village and searched the farms looking for Jews and Gypsies. Her protectors were warned by the village headman and Zekia was hidden under a haystack. She had to lie there all day without moving or coughing.

Her sister Dudija was shot by a guard when she was pushing some food through the barbed wire at Crveni Krst for her brothers. Only one brother of five survived the war.[43]

Phabol lampa
(a song from Serbia, collected by Grattan Puxon)

Phabol lampa maškar o logori (A lamp is burning in the camp)
Voi svetil amare Romenge (It shines on our Roma)
De man, Devla, dui bare phakora (O God, give me two big wings)
Te urav. Nemso te mudarav (so I can fly and kill a German)
te lav o bare nataira (and take the big keys)
Tai te putrav o Niško logor. (and open the camp at Niš.)

'The Gypsy question has been solved'

Repeated orders went to army and police units for action against Gypsies, with reminders that they assisted the partisans both as couriers and combatants. The number held at Sajmište and other centres fluctuated as extermination — speeded up by the gassing process — went on unchecked. Finally Turner reported in August 1942:

> In the interests of pacification, the Gypsy question has been fully liquidated. Serbia is the only country in which the Jewish question and the Gypsy question have been solved.

The gassing van was returned to Berlin. We estimate that several thousand Serbian Gypsies had perished by this time. But many were still alive. So why did he tell his superiors in Berlin that the Gypsy question had been 'solved'? Did he want to save the Gypsies? This is unlikely, as the killings continued in the smaller towns and villages. A more probable explanation is that he wanted to concentrate on the war against the partisans and that the morale of his soldiers was being sapped by the shooting of unarmed civilians.

SLOVENIA

Little is known about the fate of the small Gypsy community in Slovenia. We have been told that Slovene villagers hid some of the families known to them. There was at least one internment camp in Ljubljana, in a disused factory. Some Gypsies were sent to concentration camps in Croatia or deported to Germany, while others, including the Hudorović family, were deported to Tossicia camp in Italy.

Zilka Heldt recounted how her father, who had escaped to Italy, returned to Slovenia to help other Gypsies to flee. He was captured and held in the factory in Ljubljana, but, during the night, he succeeded in removing tiles from the roof and made his way back across the frontier.

VOIVODINA AND BANAT

Voivodina was occupied by the Hungarians, while Banat was placed under direct German military rule. In Voivodina, the Hungarians gave orders for the expulsion of all Gypsies not born there and these made their way to Serbia. We have no information about the fate of those who remained in Voivodina.

At one village in Banat, ninety kilometres from the capital, the Germans appointed a Gypsy named Branko to recruit workers. Between 20 and 100 were required on different occasions. The men hesitated to leave the district because they feared the Germans would believe they had gone to join the partisans and kill their families.

The work involved digging graves for Jewish victims; the Gypsies were permitted to strip the bodies and then dispose of the clothes, and received a small payment but no ration cards. Yellow armbands had to be worn and it was understood by the workers that Gypsies would follow the Jews in due course; one of the grave diggers, Dushano, recalled:

> After a month or two, they said, 'Now the partisans and the communists and the Jews are being killed, then it will be your turn.' The police told us this openly. 'It isn't time yet,' they said, 'Hitler hasn't yet fixed the day

when you'll have to be killed.' The Germans took Gypsy women to work in the barracks and they raped young girls. One day other prisoners were sent out to dig graves and we thought they were for us, so I ran away.

He crossed the frontier into Romania, was arrested on returning to Yugoslavia and sentenced to death but found himself instead doing forced labour in Austria.

GREECE

Northern Greece was at first under Bulgarian occupation, while the rest of the country was ruled by the German army, although the Germans later took over the whole of Greece. There are no reports of any centrally directed Nazi persecution of the Gypsies in Greece. Some were arrested to be used as hostages, following the practice in the neighbouring occupied territory of Serbia.

Ioannis Vrissakis was fifteen years old and working as a tinsmith some forty-five kilometres from Livadia. He was fortunate to avoid being shot as a hostage:

> There was a curfew and the Nazis came to take us away. The Captain whose name was Merer interrogated us and then told us to leave. There were five of us, my father, my brother, myself and a cousin and one other person. But a Greek came in, dressed in traditional costume, and he stamped his foot on the ground and said: No. These people must be spies because they move about.
>
> He told the Germans they should not let us go, so they put us in a store room and kept us there for three days with no food — no bread, nothing. Then they put us into trucks and took us to Livadia. There they threw us into a cell, five of us . . . There was no room to move around and we couldn't even stretch our legs. Every morning they would take us out to scrub our faces. The German SS would take pieces of brick and scrub our faces to make us look white. This misery lasted for ten days. The German SS men finally left and some soldiers from Austria came to guard us. There were 300 of us Gypsies sleeping on top of each other, eating soup from a huge boiler. Every time a German officer got killed fifty of us were taken outside and shot as hostages. When they came at night it was always to kill some of us.

Vrissakis was befriended by a Romanian called Carlos who was probably working as an interpreter for the Germans, and he arranged for Ioannis and his family to be released. They had to walk the forty-five kilometres back to their home. Ioannis spoke also of another occasion when seventeen Gypsies from Petralona were dragged out of their homes, shot and left for dead. Three in fact survived.

It is probable that the Germans in Greece were too occupied with their prime victims, the Jews, to have time for the Gypsies.

OPERATION BARBAROSSA — THE ATTACK ON THE SOVIET UNION

Germany invaded the Soviet Union in 1941 in an operation given the codename Barbarossa. It is convenient to deal with what was the Soviet Union in terms of the present-day republics, which correspond roughly to the geographical divisions at the time of the German invasion: these are the Baltic States (Estonia, Latvia, Lithuania), Belarus, Moldova, Russia and Ukraine.

First we shall look at the general policy. 'It has not yet been discovered by whom and when the order was given to kill Gypsies and Jews in the Soviet Union,' said the judges at the Nuremberg Trial of War Criminals. Nor is it possible to say with any accuracy the total number killed. We have, however, found some material which sheds light on both these questions.

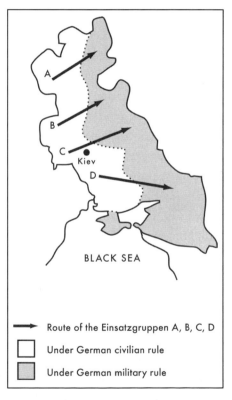

FIGURE 16. Map showing the attack on the Soviet Union

No written orders have been preserved authorising the mass killing of Gypsies and Jews in the Baltic States and the Soviet Union which took place as the Germans invaded. The Commissar Order of 6 June 1941 ordered the special treatment of Communist political commissars and the Barbarossa Jurisdiction Order gave a general right to deal harshly with the civilian population but did not in itself justify the mass murder of Gypsies and Jews.

The Task Forces

The Task Forces (*Einsatzgruppen*) were specially recruited units which had operated in Poland in 1939. They were re-established in May 1941, were active until July 1943, and were responsible for between one and two million deaths; although their records are not complete, those that have been found mention many killings of Gypsies.[44]

Altogether the Task Forces had only 3,000 members and were reinforced by the army as required for special actions. The soldiers guarded the victims prior to their execution. Units other than the Task Forces were also to kill Gypsies. The 281st Security Division shot 128 in the Novorzhev region on 7 June 1942, and the German Gendarmerie took part in killings in Kamenez-Podolsk in the Ukraine around June 1942.

At a briefing conference for the leaders of the Task Forces, Brigadier Bruno Streckenbach gave orders that 'all racially and politically undesirable elements seized who were considered dangerous to security' were to be killed. It is possible that Streckenbach did not mention Jews and Gypsies specifically but that the implication was understood by those present. Otto Ohlendorf, Commander of Task Force D, said at the trial of members of the Task Forces in 1948:

> On the basis of orders which were given to me by former Brigadier Streckenbach . . . a number of undesirable elements composed of Russians, Gypsies and Jews and others were executed in the area detailed to me.

We may note here that 'a number of undesirable elements' refers to at least 90,000 persons by the speaker's own estimate and probably half a million in truth. It seems likely that Streckenbach did not call for the killing of Jews and Gypsies on his own initiative, but that the orders originated with Heydrich, then Chief of the Security Police and Security Service. Streckenbach was to be sentenced to three years' hard labour by a Soviet war crimes court.

It is probable that Himmler announced the decision to murder the whole Jewish population of the Soviet Union during a visit to Special Unit 8 of the Task Forces in Minsk in August 1941 and that this order was interpreted as also covering any killings of Gypsies.[45] The first murders of Soviet Gypsies in fact took place in the second half of August.

The Task Forces were certainly not obliged to kill Gypsies, in particular women and children, and they must have done so for a mixture of three reasons: a generally sadistic and bloodthirsty attitude towards non-Germans; knowledge that the Gypsies were legitimate objects of persecution and could be hunted like game with the approval of their immediate and higher superiors; and indoctrination which taught that the Gypsies were an undesirable and dangerous people.

During the campaign the theoretical justification was that they were spies, partisans, helpers of the partisans, looters and so on. To some extent such a justification was needed for the ordinary soldiers, other than the Task Forces, who took part in the shootings, but it was also part of a general Nazi policy of not calling things by their right names. Thus, *Sonderbehandlung* (special treatment) was a synonym for 'execution'. It was later ordered that innocent Gypsies should be killed as well as guilty ones as they would become disaffected after their fellows had been killed. Gypsies were, of course, active in the USSR in partisan bands but the wandering tribes of men, women and children executed by the Germans could not by any stretch of the imagination be considered partisans. Ohlendorf, in his defence, used the old argument that the Gypsies were spies:

> [The Gypsies] participated in espionage organisations during campaigns . . . I want to draw your recollection to extensive descriptions of the Thirty Years War. In the Yaila mountains such activity [i.e. espionage] of Gypsies had been found.[46]

Official policy

After their occupation by the German army, Lithuania and Belarus (White Russia) came under civilian rule in September 1941, as did Estonia in December of that year. The civilian governor of this region (renamed Ostland) Hinrich Lohse issued an order to the SS and police in late December 1941:

> The Gypsies wandering around the country are a double danger.

> (i) They carry disease, especially typhus.

(ii) They are unreliable elements who cannot be put to useful work. Also they harm the German cause by passing on hostile news reports. I therefore determine that they should be treated in the same way as the Jews.

The final sentence meant a policy of extermination. The order was apparently made by Lohse at the suggestion of Georg Jedicke, Chief of Police for

```
                        Blatt 2.

                        -übertrag:                                 3 834

29.7.41 raasiniai      254 Juden, 3 lit.Communisten               257
3o.7.41 Agriogala       27    " , 11 "         "                    38
31.7.41 Utena          235    " , 16 Jüdinnen, 4 lit.Komm.
                         1 zweifacher Raubmörder                   25C
11/31.7.41 Wendziogala 13 Juden, 2 Mörder                          15

Monat August:

  1.8.41 Ukmerge        254 Juden, 42 Jüdinnen, 1 pol.Komm.
                         2 lit.NKWD-Agenten, 1 Bürgermeister
                         von Jonava, der den Befehl zum An-
                         zünden der Stadt Jonava gab               3oo
  2.8.41 Kauen-Fort    17o Juden, 1 USA-Jude, 1 USA-Jüdin,
                         33 Jüdinnen, 4 lit. Communisten           2o9
  4.8.41 Panevezys     362 Juden, 41 Jüdinnen, 5 russ.Komm.
                         14 lit.Kommunisten                        422
  5.8.41 raasiniai     213 Juden, 66 Jüdinnen                      279
  7.8.41 Uteba         483   " , 87   "  , 1 Litauer,
                         war Leichenfledderer an deutschen
                         Soldaten                                  571
  "'.8.41 Ukmerge      62o Juden, 82 Jüdinnen                      7o2
  9.8.41 Kauen-Fort    484   " , 5o   "                            534
 11.8.41 Panevezys     450   " , 48   "  , 1 lit.1 russ.K.5oo
 13.8.41 Algtus        617   " , 1oo  "  , 1 Verbrecher           719
 14.8.41 Jonava        497   " , 55   "                           552
 15.und
 16.8.41 Rokiskis      32oo Juden, Jüdinnen und J-Kinder,
                         5 lit.komm., 1 Pole, 1 Partisane         3 2o7
  9.bis
 16.8.41 raasiniai     294 Jüdinnen, 4 Judenkinder               298
 27.6.bis
 14.8.41 Rokiskis      493 Juden, 432 Russen, 56 Litauer
                         (alles aktive Kommunisten)               981
 18.8.41 Kauen-Fort IV 698 Juden, 4o2 Jüdinnen, 1 Polin,
                         711 Intell.-Juden aus dem Ghetto
                         als Repressalie für eine Sabotage-
                         Handlung                                 1 812
 19.8.41 Ukmerge       29o Juden, 255 Jüdinnen, 1 Politr.
                         88 Judenkinder, 1 russ. Kommunist        645
 22.8.41 Dünaburg      3 russ.Komm., 5 Letten, dabei war
                         1 Mörder, 1 russ.Gardist, 3 Polen,
                         3 Zigeuner, 1 Zigeunerin, 1 Zigeu-
                         nerkind, 1 Jude, 1 Jüdin, 1 Arme-
                         nier, 2 Politruks (Gefängnis-Über-
                         prüfung in Dünaburg)                      21
                                                             ─────────
                        - Uebertrag:                              16 152
```

FIGURE 17. An *Einsatzgruppe* report

the East, and was dated 4 December to justify the killing that had taken place in Libau on 5 December.

Some army officers disapproved of the shooting of Gypsies. The Commander of Army Group North had ordered, on 21 November 1941, that the shooting of Gypsies without cause should be stopped. The Task Forces, however, followed Lohse's orders and continued the killings during 1942, although the attention of at least one army unit was drawn to their Commander's order after they had killed some Gypsies in summer 1942.

In this connection we should mention a letter from the 218th Security Division to Field Command 822 in March 1943, which said that non-nomadic Gypsies who could prove a two-year period of residence in the place where they were found should be exempted from death.

The Baltic States — Task Force A

In the following pages we use the figures from Task Force records which formed part of the prosecution indictment for the post-war Trial of War Criminals in Nuremberg. Task Force A covered the Baltic States and was attached to Army Group North. Concerning their activities, we find that on 1 February 1942 units of Task Force A murdered the thirty-eight Gypsies remaining in the town of Loknya; and during the period 10 April to 24 April 1942 units of this Task Force murdered seventy-one Gypsies in Latvia. These figures represent only a fraction of some 5,000 Gypsies killed, mainly by this Task Force, in the three Baltic States.

ESTONIA

The Nazis murdered almost all the Estonian Gypsies between 1941 and 1943. Included in the massacre was the whole clan (about ninety persons) of Lajenge Roma, a distinct group from the other Estonian Gypsies, living in Lauise, about sixty-five kilometres north of Tartu.[47] Sixty Gypsies were killed in Harku concentration camp on 27 October 1942.

LATVIA

The majority of the Gypsies in Latvia were sedentary, living in their own houses or flats. Soon after the German invasion in 1941 the massacres began, with the shooting of over 100 Gypsies by German police in Libau (Lipaja). In Baltinawa Gypsies were shot alongside forty-three Jews from Bohemia. All the Gypsies in East Latvia were assembled in three towns: Ludsa, Rezenke and Vilani. At Ludsa they were locked up in a synagogue, where some died. The survivors were 'deported to the forests': that is to say, shot in the forests on 6 January 1942. In Rezenke they were shot on two consecutive nights in the same month. A total of 130 Gypsies from Vilani were killed.

Near Jelgawa 200 were shot, followed by a second group of 250–300. In Tukums 500 were killed, including the Ditschus, Gindra and Palatsch families, who were the most well known in Latvia. In Aizpute ninety Gypsies were killed and in Kuldiga 250, where some were locked up in a house and burnt alive.

Gypsies were also shot in Hargla, Ligatne, Venspils and Wlamiera. In the last named town the nine members of the Sinanis family, from grandparents to grandchildren, were killed. In Baukas district 250 Gypsies were brought together and shot. In Talsen district, however, Mayor Kruminsch protected the Gypsies. On his orders none were killed and the grateful Gypsies were later to erect a monument over his grave. The situation in Daugawpils is less clear. It seems as if an order to spare the Gypsies there came too late for many.

In the massacres of 1941–2 between 1,500 and 2,000 were killed, about a third of the Gypsy population, but in 1943 the situation was to change after new instructions from Himmler. Killings stopped and surviving Gypsies were forcibly called up into the German army to fight the Soviet forces. Many deserted and one who was recaptured was imprisoned for six months. Vanya Kochanowski has recounted how he was conscripted and after many adventures ended up as a forced labourer in France. Here he escaped and was helped to hide by French Gypsies.[48]

LITHUANIA

The only published reference to Lithuania we have found is to the arrival of a transport of twenty persons at Auschwitz. It seems likely, however, that the majority of Lithuanian Gypsies suffered the same fate as those of Estonia and Latvia.

BELARUS

At the time of the German attack on the Soviet Union the Gypsy population of Belarus was some 17,000, almost all sedentary. There were five Gypsy schools, run by the Belarus Gypsy Union, with teachers who had been trained at the Gypsy Teachers Training College in Russia. Five collective farms had been set up.

Into this peaceful community came the invading German army and the Task Forces. Many Gypsies were among the 200,000 victims at the concentration camp at Trastiniets, near Minsk. At Pastovi, near Vitebsk, twenty-eight nomadic families were executed. It is estimated that some 6,000 in all were killed before the civilian German government ordered a stop to the killings of the sedentaries.

Deportation to concentration camps continued. These included two small transports to Auschwitz — twenty persons from Grodno and Orel (28 November 1943) and eighteen from Vitebsk. We do not know whether these were nomadic or sedentary Gypsies.

Two hundred Belarus Gypsies served in the Soviet army. Some thirty were decorated, including Ivan Pasevitch from Tolochin, who was captain of an infantry company. Another Gypsy, Sergej Kotslowski, was an admiral in the Soviet fleet. Many other Gypsies, along with their families, joined the partisans in the forests of Brest, Minsk and Vitebsk.

Himmler decides

In June 1942 the Minister for the Eastern Occupied Territories had written to Lohse from Berlin asking for information on the Gypsies in order to establish a general policy. In May 1943 Lohse put forward his proposals for dealing with the Gypsies to Himmler, the Nazi Party, the Army and the Governors of Ostland (the three Baltic States with Belarus) and the Ukraine. He proposed that the Gypsies should be put in special camps and settlements. They should not however 'be treated as Jews' (i.e. be killed). No distinction was to be made between nomadic and sedentary Gypsies. Part-Gypsies should generally be treated as Gypsies.

A final decision was held up awaiting Himmler's approval. He modified the proposals, exempting the sedentary Gypsies but condemning the nomads to death. Himmler's Order of 15 November 1943 (published in December of that year) reads:

(i) Sedentary Gypsies and part-Gypsies are to be treated as citizens of the country.

(ii) Nomadic Gypsies and part-Gypsies are to be placed on the same level as Jews and placed in concentration camps.

The police commanders will decide in cases of doubt who is a Gypsy.

This official distinction between sedentaries and nomads was only made in Belarus and the Baltic states and little weight should be placed on it when assessing long-term Nazi intentions towards the Gypsies. In other occupied countries in central and eastern Europe there was no such distinction. It came too late, of course, for several hundred settled Gypsies who had already been killed. Some sedentary Gypsies in the Baltic states were then drafted to serve the Nazis in labour brigades and isolated cases are also known of their being sent to concentration camps in spite of Himmler's instructions.

RUSSIA

Occupied Russia remained under German military command and those Gypsies who had not managed to flee to the east were seen as targets until the Soviet army began to hold up and then drive back the Nazi troops from 1943.

Here we turn again to the records of the Task Forces. Task Force B covered the Moscow region and was attached to Army Group Centre. We find in their monthly reports:

During the period 6 March to 30 March 1942 in the vicinity of Klincy Special Unit 7a of Task Force B killed 45 Gypsies, while in the same period in the vicinity of Mogilev Task Commando 8 killed 33 Gypsies.

As in the case of the Baltic states, the reports that have survived are incomplete and indicative only.

Smolensk, where many hundreds of Gypsies were killed, was in the region covered by Task Force B. The dead included 1,000 Gypsies shot and buried alive at Rodnya, near Smolensk. Tractors were used to push the earth down over the still-living victims. There is a monument in Smolensk with the names of the victims of the fascists; many Gypsy names can be seen on it. The actor Sergei Leonov, of the Moscow Gypsy Theatre (Teater Romen), lost seven members of his family there. The Gypsy Theatre toured during the war period and gave 600 concerts for Red Army soldiers. Two of the actors, Sergei Zolotaryov and Viktor Belyakov, joined the Soviet armed forces and were decorated for bravery in battle.

At one collective farm, where all the workers were Gypsies, the Germans shot the president, Andrej Massalskij, and sent the Gypsies to the ghetto of Roslav.

Many Gypsies were killed in Kiev. Task Force C covered the area and was attached to Army Group South. Regarding their activities, the Nuremberg Tribunal stated:

> In September or October 1941 in the vicinity of Vyrna and Dederev Special Commando 4a murdered 32 Gypsies.

Another report collected for the Tribunal (NO-2827) said:

> In November 1941 414 Gypsies were killed by Task Force C.

Task Force D covered south Russia, south Ukraine and the Crimea and was attached to the 11th Army. Again from the Tribunal indictment:

> During the period 16 February to 28 February 1942 Task Force D murdered 421 Gypsies.
> During the period 1 March to 15 March 1942 the Task Force murdered 810 Gypsies.
> During the period 15 March to 30 March 1942 the Task Force murdered 261 Gypsies.

Klincy

Evidence given at post-war trials expanded the brief report of the forty-five Gypsies killed in Klincy, cited above. In March 1942 some 30 Gypsies and 270 Jews were killed there. They were brought in lorries to the side of a ditch where their money and outer clothes were taken off them. Then they were shot in groups in front of those waiting their turn for execution.

In spring 1942 a group of some ten to fifteen Gypsies came into Klincy with horses and carts. They were arrested by a Task Force unit and orders were given for them to receive 'special treatment'. They were shot in the neck at the edge of a trench. The Commander of the unit, Karl Matschke, was to be sentenced in 1966 to five years in prison for this and another shooting.

'Exterminate these bands'

In 1942 pressure to kill Gypsies in occupied parts of Russia increased. A report from the Chiefs of the Army Field Police on the development of the partisan movement was sent to all Army Groups on 25 August 1942. It contained, among other items, the following recommendation:

> The appearance of Gypsy bands is a major threat to the pacification of the territory as their members are roaming the country as beggars and render many services to the partisans, providing them with supplies etc. If only part of those Gypsies who are suspected or convicted of being partisan supporters were punished, the attitude of the remainder would be even more hostile towards the German forces and support the partisans even more than before. It is necessary to exterminate these bands ruthlessly.

A survivor's story

Soviet sources dealing with German atrocities do not normally mention whether the persons concerned were Jews or Gypsies, but a few survivors, such as Valentin Ivanov, have told their story.

Valentin Ivanov was born in 1930 in Ostrov (Pskov region). His parents were sedentary and even after the arrival of the Germans he continued to attend school together with Russian children. Then in 1943 the Germans collected all the Gypsies in Ostrov and took them to a camp nearby. A few months later they were taken to another camp near Saulkrasti in Latvia. Here the parents were separated from the children and transported to another camp. Gypsy children were kept in a separate barracks in Saulkrasti but none were killed. The guards used to beat them and one Russian guard threw cigarettes among the children for them to fight over and poured water over them as they were struggling on the floor. The Gypsy children were then taken to the special Gypsy camp at Konstantynow, near Lodz. This was the children's branch of the Lodz ghetto camp. In 1944 Valentin was taken with other Gypsy boys to Auschwitz and three months later to Mauthausen, where he stayed until the camp was liberated by the Russians. His mother was in Stutthof camp and was among some thirty Ostrov Gypsies who survived the war. His father never returned.

It has also been said that Gypsy children were deported by the Germans from the Leningrad area, but nothing is known of their fate. On the other hand, some children from besieged Leningrad itself were saved from starvation by being evacuated to Sweden. The civil rights worker Aleka Stubin was one of these.

UKRAINE

The Ukraine, like Russia, remained under German military rather than civilian rule throughout the war and indiscriminate slaughter was practised.

The Germans occupied Simferopol in November 1941. Gypsies had been settled in the town since 1874; their cultural club had 300 members. The Nazis lost no time in destroying this community. The Commander of the 2nd Army told the Chief of Commando 11b (part of Task Force D) that they expected his unit to kill several thousand Jews and Gypsies by Christmas that year. In fact, 824 Gypsies were dead before 15 December. This was confirmed by an exchange that took place at the Nuremberg Trials.

> Prosecutor: When were the Jews, Krimchak Jews and Gypsies executed in Simferopol?
> Braune: In the first half of December 1941.

Task Force report no. 152 of 9 January 1942 had simply said that 'in Simferopol the Gypsy problem has been cleared up'.

In the village of Ungut all the Gypsies were shot. The Gypsies in Asan-Bey were locked in a storehouse and when a delegation of three older Crimean Tatars asked the German commander to free them the officer said he would only release them if the Tatars were willing to die in their place. The Gypsies were then shot. In the village of Krasnye Yerchi all the Gypsies were shot except one ten-year-old, who was hidden in the Tatar quarter. More than 100 Gypsies were killed in the village of Duma-Eli.

Babi Yar

In the course of two days, 29–30 September 1941, German Nazis aided by their collaborators murdered 33,771 Jewish civilians in a ravine at Babi Yar in Kiev. In the months that followed, thousands more Jews and others were seized and taken to the ravine, where they were shot. It is estimated that more than 100,000 people, including Gypsies, were executed by the Nazis there during the Second World War.

The Russian author Yevgeni Kuznetsov wrote:

> It is known that in the Ukraine the Gypsies were victims of the same massive immediate destruction as the Jews. The passport was of decisive importance. They examined the passports in the streets, they examined

them when they searched houses. Physical appearance was in second place. People with black eyes and hair, with a long nose, did their best not to show themselves in the street. The Gypsies were led to Babi Yar [to be killed] by entire camps and, apparently, until the last moment they did not understand what was going to be done to them.

The 1926 census in the USSR showed 60,000 Gypsies, of whom 42,000 lived in the European part of the Soviet Union. By the time of the Nazi invasion in 1941 there could have been 60,000 in the area which was to come under German control. We estimate that up to 30,000 were killed in Belarus, Russia and the Ukraine.

IN THE SHADOW
OF THE SWASTIKA:

GERMANY'S ALLIES AND PUPPET STATES

Germany's allies in Europe and the puppet states of Croatia and Slovakia were able to decide their own policy on Gypsies. These varied from comparative tolerance in Bulgaria to genocide in Croatia. Although Finland was an ally of Germany, no measures were taken against its Gypsy population.

ALBANIA

The Italian authorities who controlled Albania seemed no more anxious to attack the Gypsies there than they had those in Italy itself. The Gypsies apparently continued a peaceable existence throughout the Second World War, although there is a story that some were deported to an island in the Adriatic. Some Albanian Gypsies did join the partisans from January 1943 onwards.

BULGARIA

The fascist press in Bulgaria attacked the Gypsy community, which numbered well over 100,000 in 1939. It was claimed that the control and police supervision of Gypsies had cost the state five hundred million leva (about £500,000 at that time) and that this was a waste of money.

In May 1942 a decree was issued saying that Gypsies would be made to do forced labour in public works. In August that year marriages between Bulgarians and Gypsies were forbidden and, later, instructions were issued that Gypsies as well as Jews would receive lower rations than Bulgarians.

The government announced in May 1943 that all 'idle' Gypsies aged from sixteen to fifty would be mobilised for the harvest. Raids were made on coffee houses and inns and in August that year the newspaper *Dnes* reported that thousands of Gypsies had already been deported from the capital and many more would follow.

Although no Romanies were deported to concentration camps from Bulgaria, Gypsies were placed in camps there together with Jews. There had already been some intermarriage between these groups before the war and many friendships grew in the camps. After the liberation from the fascists most of these mixed couples married and migrated to Israel.

The German Ambassador in Sofia, Adolf Beckerle, advised the German Foreign Office in June 1943 that there were difficulties in obtaining agreement with the Bulgarian authorities on the deportation of Jews. The reason, he said, was that 'the Bulgarians have lived for too long with peoples like Armenians, Greeks and Gypsies to appreciate the Jewish problem'.[49]

Partisans

Sedentary Gypsies from smaller towns were called up to the Bulgarian army. However, others joined the partisans or were *Yataks*, the name given to those who helped the partisans by hiding them or supplying them with food.

Dimiter Nemtsov, from Sliven, was in the Bulgarian occupying forces in Macedonia. He deserted and joined the partisans. Yusein Kamenov was killed as a partisan in Bulgaria in 1944. Velichka Drumcheva, from Gabrovo, was executed as a *Yatak*, as were Mustafa Yuchev and Yusein Musov, both from the Vratsa region. Seven Gypsies were killed and two imprisoned after the September Anti-Fascist Revolt in 1944. Altogether some twenty Gypsies were hailed after the war as active fighters against the fascist Bulgarian government.

It is said that, when Jews from Bulgarian-occupied Greece arrived in a train at Lom on their way to the death camps, Bulgarian Gypsies helped to give them food.

CROATIA AND BOSNIA

Within days of the German conquest of Yugoslavia in April 1941 Croatia was set up as a puppet state. It included Bosnia and parts of Serbia. The leader of the government was Ante Pavelić, who had set up the ultra-nationalist Ustasha party in 1929.

Few Gypsies survived the terror in Croatia itself. The Catholic-supported Ustasha took power four days after German units crossed the frontier and inaugurated a bloodbath. The victims died in what was popularly termed a 'holy war' against non-Catholic minorities: the Serbs, who were Orthodox Christians, and the Jews, to whom the Gypsies were added regardless of their religion.

In July 1941 the Minister of Internal Affairs ordered a census of all the Gypsies on its territory. The lists of names were to be returned to the Ministry by the end of the month. A Gypsy had been defined earlier as 'a person descending from two ancestors of the second degree of kinship belonging to the Gypsy race' — that is, having two Romany grandparents. Notices went up everywhere in public places, in offices, shops and cafes, proclaiming 'No Serbs, Jews, Nomads or dogs allowed'.

The Minister of Justice and Religion Dr Puk issued an order in November that same year that 'undesirable persons' could be sent by force to collectives and labour camps. These camps were to be run by the fascist militia, known as the Ustashi, which formed the strong arm of the administration. Gypsies in Croatia, numbering some 28,000, became their prey on religious as well as racial grounds, as most professed the Orthodox faith. The Muslim Gypsies of Bosnia were largely spared because the Muslim leaders, based in Sarajevo, protected them.

Zilka's story

From the account given by Zilka Heldt we know of the panic and desperation that seized families as they sought to escape capture and death. Yugoslavia was criss-crossed by different civilian and military authorities, each imposing its own controls. Zilka's aunt Helenka, caught in the street, was pushed into the back of a truck along with her children, and never again seen by her relatives. The round-ups went on everywhere and Gypsy families moved cautiously from one village to another:

> We kept to the woods as much as possible but had to go to houses for food sometimes. Some Gypsies were sheltered by peasants they knew or who took pity on us.

Of those who headed for the frontiers, a few reached the comparative safety of Italy, while others ended in the concentration camp near Zemun (Semlin), outside Belgrade. Although given shelter by the Italian local authorities, Zilka Heldt's parents twice went back into Yugoslavia to seek relatives. But most had already perished or were in hiding in the remoter mountains of Bosnia and Serbia, from where the men eventually joined the partisans.

Murders outside the camps

The reports by survivors from Croatia tell of murder and torture. Ustashi militiamen took hold of young children and beat them to death against the trees. One atrocity, described by Angela Hudorović, concerned the death of her sister and young niece. First the girl was forced to dig a ditch while her mother, seven months' pregnant, was left tied to a tree. They opened the belly of the mother with a knife, took out the baby and threw it into the ditch. Then they raped the girl and threw her in the ditch with her mother. They covered them with earth while they were still alive.

One large family, the Wittes, had fled into Croatia in a bid to get away from Germany. Thirty-four members crossed the frontier, only to be taken by the Ustashi. After brutal mistreatment they were locked in a barn and burnt alive. The incident was recorded by a priest from the nearby village of Marija Sorica.

Arrests and massacre

The documentation prepared for the trial of Andrija Artuković — the Croatian Minister for Internal Affairs — reveals the full story of massacres in Croatia. Gypsies were rounded up in each town and village and the majority deported to the concentration camp at Jasenovac. The first transport of Gypsies, of 300 persons from Zagreb, was on 29 April 1941.

In April 1942 all the Gypsies living in the villages of Jamnica and Tomic — a total of eighty — were arrested by the police and Ustashi. On the day the Gypsies were arrested more than forty villagers went to see the District Chief to protest against the arrest of the Gypsies. The villagers wanted them set free and returned to their homes. The District Chief wrote to Artuković pleading for the release of the Gypsies, describing their good relationships and the ways in which they had helped the farmers. The Minister never replied. The eighty were sent to Zagreb and then to Jasenovac. None returned.

The Gypsies from Brod na Savi were packed in eighty-three cattle trucks: about 2,000 persons in all. Their houses were sealed and their horses were given to Croats. The poultry and pigs were sold at auction and the proceeds put in the local treasury. Their empty houses and land were also given to Croats.

Muslim Gypsies

In July 1941 a delegation of Muslim Gypsies from Bijeljina went to complain to the Islamic religious authorities in Sarajevo about the discrimination, and at a conference in Sarajevo later that month the Ustashi genocide of Muslim Gypsies was condemned. A commission was set up to prepare a document defending the Muslim Gypsies. The members were Dervis Korku, from the local museum, Hamdija Kresejaković and Muhammed Kantardzić, academics, and Hadzi Mehmed Hadzić, a writer and theologian. In the document they wrote that the Muslim Gypsies should be considered members of the Muslim community and that an attack on them would be considered as an attack on the Muslim community itself.

The policy of the Nazi rulers in Germany was to cultivate the friendship of the Muslims in the Middle East and the puppet Croatian leaders tried not to antagonise the many Muslims in that country. They agreed to the propositions of the Islamic religious authorities in Sarajevo:

> It has been ordered that the so-called white Gypsies — Muslims — must not be touched as these must be considered to be Aryan. Thus no measures whatsoever must be applied to them, even orders to be implemented against Gypsies.

So read an official document, probably emanating from the Ministry for the Interior in Zagreb in August 1941. The Ustashi Supervision Service sent orders to Sarajevo in June 1942 warning that some non-Muslim Gypsies were beginning to wear fezzes to avoid deportation to camps.

The lists of deportees from Dubrava (Kozara region), Rovine, and Mokrice to the camps at Jasenovac, Stara Gradiška and Strug, however, contain Muslim names: Ibrahim Mahmutt Alimanović, Fatima Alija Halilović, Hasan Kasim Kahrić, Fatima Bego Kahrić, Ibrahim Serif Omerović, and Ibresa Mahmujt Sarić.

The small number of Catholic Gypsies did not get this protection from their Church and those from Glina and elsewhere were killed.

Jasenovac concentration camp

Toma Djorjević arrived at Jasenovac on 2 June 1942. The train stopped outside the camp. Here the guards took everything he and the other Gypsies had, including the food they had taken for the journey. An officer with a gun came and told the Gypsies to surrender all their money and gold and that if anything was found afterwards they would be shot on the spot.

A few Gypsies were set to work in Camp IIIC, named the Gypsy Camp. The rest were exterminated on or shortly after arrival. Those Gypsies spared for labour had to work in the brick factory and the sawmill, and dig irrigation canals. In time, they were also killed through beatings or died of hunger and exhaustion. The Gypsies lived in tents or under the open sky, hungry and barefoot in sun and rain alike. The food given to them was worse than that given to the other inmates and the Ustashi took special pleasure in beating and whipping them. Then at night they would take some out of the camp to be killed. In any case, conditions in Camp IIIC were so bad that on many a morning up to forty bodies of prisoners who had died of the cold were removed from the camp.

Some of the Gypsies who came to Jasenovac were musicians and the Ustashi created several groups of Gypsy players. In June 1942 the Gypsies and other prisoners were forced to put on a concert. Then they were murdered. Some non-Gypsies, however, tried to hide Gypsies from the Ustashi.

FIGURE 18. Jasenovac camp

FIGURE 19. Mass grave at Jasenovac

FIGURE 20. Railway line leading to Jasenovac

One such Gypsy was a violinist called Jovanović. But the Camp Commander Filipović discovered him and had him killed. The camp hospital was not allowed to accept Gypsies. The Ustashi priest, nicknamed Father Satan, ordered that any sick Gypsies were to be killed.

Bozidar F. worked in the camp laundry; he had been able to conceal his identity. Another Gypsy — a violinist called Vaso — played in the camp orchestra. Together with two German Gypsies from Thuringia who had worked in a fair as fire-eaters, they were the only Gypsies still alive in the last days of the camp.

Extermination at Ustice and Gradina

A survivor, Dusan Culum, related how mass killings took place at Ustice, on the other side of the river from Jasenovac. Every day six to twelve wagon-loads of Gypsies would arrive at Jasenovac. They would disembark from the train in front of the camp, where they had to sit on the ground. Camp Commander Luburic or other Ustashi officers would tell them they were going to be settled on the land to work. The Ustashi would first take away the men, telling them they would be sent as labourers to Germany and making them sing 'Blessed be Pavelić's head' as they were marched off. The guards took them in rafts across the river to Ustice and put them in houses whose Serbian owners had been killed, which were surrounded by wire, forming a small camp. Then the Ustashi killed the Gypsies with mallets and buried them in the gardens. After killing the men they would come back and kill the women and children.

Another group were told on arrival they would be sent to Bosnia to settle the land of partisans who had fled to the forest. 'God bless you,' said a Gypsy woman when she heard this. These Gypsies were then all driven on to rafts and carried across the river to Ustice. The men were taken to the edge of the river, tied up in groups of five and killed. The Ustashi then came back once again to kill the women and children.

When the capacity of the annihilation camp at Ustice was not enough to cope with the number of prisoners arriving in Jasenovac, a new extermination centre was opened at nearby Gradina. One group was taken straight from the train to Gradina — men, women and children — without going through Jasenovac camp. They were ordered to sing wedding songs as they marched. On arrival at Gradina they were executed and buried in ditches.

Another survivor describes how one transport of women and children was brought by barge to Gradina, where some prisoners had already dug a ditch. The women were brought towards the ditch in a group and then taken individually to the edge of the ditch, where they were killed. When the ditch was full of bodies it was covered with earth. Then the work party dug another ditch. The murdered Gypsies' clothes were sent to a rag factory in the camp and from there to a factory in Zagreb owned by a Croat, Pripic.

Some Gypsies were used as gravediggers. At intervals the members of these work parties were killed and a new group formed. In 1945 the last party of gravediggers was murdered so that no witnesses would be left.

Escape from Jasenovac

Simon Kotur was a member of a gravedigging brigade from Camp IIIC. He managed to escape and later recounted:

> Some of us were selected to be replaced by new gravediggers. We had our hands bound and were loaded on the raft to cross the river Sava. We could see another group of Gypsies on the other side, digging graves for us. They shouted to us: You won't be killed tonight. We haven't been able to make enough room for you all.
>
> All that day we watched them digging our graves. My friend Branko said: They are going to kill us tomorrow. We have to escape somehow. We agreed that, as the Ustashi began to drive us towards the ditches, we would jump on them and run. The Ustashi killed twenty of the group that evening. The next day we watched while the other Gypsies dug graves till midday. At 4 P.M. these Gypsies brought us under Ustashi escort a pot of stew. Three hours later those who had eaten the food fell to the ground in convulsions and died. At 9 P.M. the Ustashi started to collect the rest of us. We were told to undress. Stevo jumped on an Ustashi and shouted: Children run! I was able to get over the wire and ran towards where the Una river joins the Sava. Four of us managed to escape and run through the fields to Prodsara.

Joka Nikolić was another who escaped just before being killed and hid in the reeds by the river. Later he joined the partisans. Here he met up with another escapee from Jasenovac, Janko Gommen. After several such escapes the Gypsies were kept under guard with machine guns and wired together in pairs as they were being led to the slaughter.

Many forms of death

In July 1942 Gypsies were brought from other camps, including Stara Gradiška, to Jasenovac. The trains, with the victims on board, would often stand for days outside the camp and the women and children, with no food or water, died. They carried out bodies from the cars. Any survivors were taken under the Ustashi's whips to their death in Gradina.

In Jasenovac one Gypsy was ordered to kill another. Instead, he threw away the stick and impaled himself on the barbed-wire fence. On another day an inmate saw Ustashi throwing small children up in the air and catching them on their bayonets. Sometimes Gypsy women waiting to be shot would jump into the Sava with their babies and drown themselves.

Dragutin Pudić

Dragutin Pudić had been responsible for many killings in Jadovna, a camp for Jews and Serbs. Then he came to Jasenovac. He wanted to make sure the number of Gypsies killed each day equalled the number of new arrivals, as he was afraid that if too many Gypsies were in the camp they might rebel. He would walk about the camp with a revolver and would sometimes turn swiftly and shoot the nearest prisoner. In Gradina he would select the prettiest Gypsy women and rape them before they were killed.

One day a two-year-old started crying. Pudić said, 'OK. So, you don't want me to cut your throat.' He then placed the girl and other children in sacks and threw them alive into the ditch. Pudić laughed and then shouted at the Gypsy gravediggers: 'Cover them up, you idiots.'

How many were killed?

No records were kept of Gypsy arrivals at Jasenovac. But the census lists show how many were taken from each village and in each case only one or two survived. Long lists of names, place by place, ranging from tens to hundreds, can be found in the documentation by Bulajić cited here.[50]

Estimates for the number of Gypsies killed in Bosnia range between 25,000 and 30,000; the majority met their death at the Djakovo camp or Jasenovac.[51]

HUNGARY

Nationalists in Hungary were no friends to the Gypsies but persecution did not begin in earnest until the fascist Arrow Cross movement took power in 1944.

In 1934 Laszlo Endre, who later became the Secretary of State responsible for organising the deportation of Jews to concentration camps, had already demanded that itinerant Gypsies be sent to state concentration camps and the men sterilised. In February 1941 György Forster, an MP for the Party of Hungarian Life, proposed the setting-up of labour camps for all nomadic Gypsies. A newspaper pointed out that the Gypsies cost the country seventy-five million pengös (about ten million pounds at the time) a year in handling and supervision, as much as the Hungarian Diplomatic Corps.

Leading Hungarian personalities expressed their horror at intermarriage between Gypsies and non-Gypsies and the subsequent production of a stratum of half-castes, but an attempt to prohibit such marriages by Professor Ferenc Orsös in July 1941 was defeated in the Upper House of the Parliament. In June 1942, however, the Budapest Chamber of Agriculture proposed the sterilisation of all Gypsy males.

In February 1941 the Hungarian government made plans to intern in work camps all Gypsies without a profession, but this was not carried out throughout Hungary. Discrimination against Gypsies seems to have taken place at a low level on local initiative as long as Hungary remained independent. Work camps were set up in a few places, some authorities placed restrictions on the Gypsies in their areas, and some counties later took away their ration cards.

Hungary enters the war

After Hungary entered the Second World War as an ally of Germany in June 1941 Gypsies and other ethnic minority men were conscripted into the army alongside Hungarians. They were sent to the eastern front where many were killed or captured.

Meanwhile, in many towns their relatives were herded into ghettos. The first ghetto for Gypsies was set up in Nagyszalonta in 1941, well before Jews were collected in ghettos. At Estergom a closed quarter was set up for every Gypsy family. They could only leave the quarter for work and were not allowed to sit on public benches in the main town. A ghetto created in Révfalu in 1944 collected together 1,000 Gypsies from the town and the surrounding Szigetvár area. Those with flats had them confiscated and were then interned as itinerants.

Labour camps

Persecution of Jews and Gypsies on a wider scale began in 1944, when the Germans occupied Hungary. From March 1944 they began deporting Jews, with attention turning to the Gypsies later in the year as the Germans strengthened their hold over the Hungarian government and the Arrow Cross movement took control of the central government.

In August 1944 the Defence Ministry ordered the setting-up of Gypsy labour brigades. All males aged between sixteen and sixty who were not in the army were conscripted into these unarmed units. Digging trenches to stop the advancing Soviet forces was a prime task. This was the first order from central government affecting the Gypsies and some local authorities resisted the enrolling of Gypsies in the brigades as they wanted them to help with the harvest, but German and Hungarian soldiers and police rounded up the Gypsies from the settlements in the areas which had not yet been occupied by the advancing Soviet army. There are reports of Gypsies being sent to labour brigade camps from Baranya, Somogy and many other districts. Anyone escaping from a labour camp would be treated as an army deserter and shot.

Deportations

The Arrow Cross party took power in October 1944 and shortly afterwards Gypsies were forbidden to leave their place of residence and had to carry a residence permit with them. It is likely that this was — as had happened earlier in Germany — a preliminary move before deportation to camps in Poland.

Figures from the Heves region collected by György Meszaros give an idea of the extent of the deportation from there:

> Andornaktalya-Felso: Most of the forty families hid in the forests. About twenty persons did not return from deportation, including the daughter of the informant.

> Eger (Veroszala Street): Only one man was taken by the Germans and he did not return. The others (forty families) hid in the forest.

> Kerescend: Twenty-two men out of some 100 in the town were sent to a Collecting Camp at Mezökövesd and then to Germany or Poland and about ten did not return.

Tiszaigar: 'Many' taken to Mezökövesd.

From Mezökövesd and similar collecting camps in other parts of Hungary Gypsies were taken — often on foot — to Komárom on the border and then deported to Germany or Poland. In Komárom several thousand Gypsies passed through two old fortresses used as transit centres. Some remained there in poor conditions for weeks before being sent on to concentration camps.

Eyewitness accounts

Kallai Janos has told how he escaped on a forced march out of Hungary:

> In the district of Heves about 700 male Gypsies were collected together in Mezökövesd. They came from the villages of Andornaktalya-Felso, Bogacs and Kal, as well as from Mezökövesd itself. The males were collected in Laszlo school, and the women and children at another place. All had to work. First we worked in the fields and then building trenches. We were guarded by Germans and Hungarian Pfeilkreuzler [Arrow Cross] soldiers. Particularly cruel were Sergeant Karoly Toth and Lieutenant Dezso Ujlaki. We stayed about four weeks in the camp during which time about 300 of the Gypsies escaped. In the camp the soldiers took everything away from everybody. They said they would shoot anyone who didn't give up his papers and soldier's book. In spite of that I didn't give up my soldier's book. I had been a soldier in 1941–3 on the Russian front.
>
> From Mezökövesd we marched to Tiszapolgar, the men separately from the women and children. But the Russians were already firing at the village and we were sent back to Egarszalok, then Eger Visonta, Gyongyos and Nagymaros. At Nagymaros we crossed the Danube and made a forced march to Komárom and Györ. The soldiers, who travelled in a horse-drawn cart, told us we must reach Germany within a week. From Nagymaros we marched together with the Jews. We were distinguished from the Jews by a yellow ribbon on our arm. Anyone who became ill during the march was shot by the German soldiers. I and my friend Adam Paczok fled before Györ.
>
> I was the coachman of the string of wagons which carried the German soldiers' property. The soldiers trusted me and when one soldier's horse was lame because the shoe had fallen off he said to me: 'Kallai, go to a

blacksmith in the village and get a horseshoe made. But if you don't come back within two hours we will shoot you like a dog.'

I found a blacksmith in the village and I left the horse there telling the blacksmith that I had to go and get food for the horse. I didn't return but went by a roundabout route to the forest and there I met other Gypsies. Of the 400 Gypsies who left Mezökövesd on the march only ten to fifteen succeeded in fleeing. I don't know where in Germany the others were taken but no one I knew came back.

Another eyewitness, Ilona Raffael, was deported to Germany and survived the death march when the SS evacuated the prisoners from Ravensbrück on foot to Dachau. She recounts:

In autumn 1944 a list was made of all the Gypsies in Adacs, the men aged sixteen to sixty and the women from sixteen to forty. In November we were deported by German soldiers. Only about seventy Gypsies were taken as after the lists were made many fled from the village. First we went to Hatvan where we were put in the Jewish synagogue. From there we went with our families to Komárom. There we were put into the town prison and the men and women separated. The men were taken somewhere in Germany, the women and the girls were taken first of all to Ravensbrück and then to Dachau. We had to work all the time, in Ravensbrück we worked in the sand mine.

We were together with Polish, German, Hungarian and Russian Jewesses. Our clothes were a blue and white striped dress, on our feet were wooden sandals. The Germans cut off all our hair. On the left arm of our dress the number of the barrack was sewn with green numbers on a white background. My barrack number was 19. Many Gypsy women and girls died in Ravensbrück but I do not know how many. Those who could not work were shot by German soldiers. When the Russian soldiers approached we marched to Dachau. During the journey many women were shot as they could not walk any further. At Dachau the Russians liberated us. Of my family the following died — Ferenc, aged sixty, Istvan, aged forty-six, Ferenc, aged twenty-one, and Laszlo, aged nineteen.

Karoly Lendvai was living in Szentgal when Hungarian police descended on the town and forced twelve Gypsy families to walk seventy-two kilometres to Komárom. He described how he escaped on the journey from Komárom to a concentration camp:

> As we marched through villages others joined our group, more Gypsies and more police. Some babies died on the way and some who attempted to escape were shot and left by the roadside. We were in Komárom about two weeks with hardly any food and water was scarce. Many people died as typhus broke out and others were killed. The dead were thrown into a huge pit and covered with quicklime.
>
> One day we were herded into cattle wagons to be taken I don't know where. 'Rot, you Jew-Gypsy,' screamed an Arrow Cross guard at me as we were shoved into the train. Suddenly there were sirens and bombs were falling. The wagon I was in was damaged and some of us escaped. We hid in the woods for about a year until the war ended.

Deportations also took place from the counties of Baranya, Vas, Veszprem and Zala. No central decree has been found to order these deportations and it is likely that they were taken on the initiative of the local fascist authorities.

The Ghetto room at Komárom
(a song from Hungary, collected by Klara Majoros)

The ghetto room in Komárom
Every Gypsy knows it
And tell their families crying
Oh, how the ghetto room stinks.

I'm in the ghetto
They've shaved my head
Oh my God, what am I to do?
Shall I run or shall I stay?
If I run they'll shoot me
If I stay they'll beat me to death.

In concentration camps

No one knows yet how many Hungarian Gypsies were sent to Germany and Poland. Nor do we have records to show where all the deportees were sent. It was estimated by one organisation after the war that some 3,000 persons returned from Germany and Poland, but there are no accurate figures for the number who were transported there. Mezey estimated that the figure was 30,000.[52] One problem is that Gypsies with Hungarian nationality or names were also arrested in the Austrian Burgenland.

The incomplete records of Natzweiler camp show that five Gypsies who died there on 7 January 1945 had Hungarian Gypsy names: Geza Balog, Sandor Bogdan, Laszlo Raffael and Ivan Sztojka. The fifth, Jozsef Gazsi, was a sedentary Gypsy from Hungary. Joska Nyari of the Budapest settlement (behind Vizmellek Street) was taken to Berga-Elster after the Budapest Jews had been deported and died there of illness in the winter of 1944/5. The presence of Hungarian Gypsies in Gross-Rosen has also been recorded but the fate of the majority of Hungarian Gypsies after their deportation still represents one of the gaps in the documentation.

The final months

As the front line in the east approached many Gypsies were murdered on the spot — in Lengyel, Lenti and Varalja. The killings went on until the end. After the German army had temporarily recaptured some territory from the Russians, 150 Gypsies — men, women and children — were killed in the Varpalota forest on the grounds that they had helped the Red Army.

On 23 February 1945 Gabor Vajna, the Arrow Cross Interior Minister, announced, 'I have begun to make draconian arrangements which the behaviour of these alien races [Jews and Gypsies] has made necessary.' Following this, new camps were set up at Keled, at Nagykanizsa (in a coffee factory) and elsewhere. It seems that, had the war continued, the Gypsies would have suffered the fate of the Hungarian Jews.

HUNGARIAN-OCCUPIED SLOVAKIA

Hungary occupied part of Slovakia as early as 1938. Arpad Krok, from Košice, relates that his father was sent to a work-camp in Transylvania (which had also been annexed by Hungary). He and his three brothers found themselves in the concentration camp for Gypsies and Jews at Komárom. Their living quarters were underground and the lice were so numerous that, as he describes it, 'the children threw handfuls at each other'. As he was only twelve, Arpad was in the women's camp. On one occasion he saw the guards shoot a new-born baby and its mother. The baby died immediately and the mother some days later, apparently from gangrene in the untreated wound in her breast. Later Arpad and his family were sent to Dachau.

Ludovic Bihari from Rastice told how the Nyilashi (Hungarian fascists) caught him and put a rope around his chest. They tied the other end to a horse's saddle and he was dragged along the ground. He was then sent to Mauthausen, where he spent twenty-eight months. On his lower leg he still carried a large scar from medical experiments performed on him in the camp before he escaped.

Andr'oda taboris
(a song from Czechoslovakia, collected by Milena Hübschmannová)

Andr'oda taboris (In that camp)
phares buti keren. (they work hard.)
Phares buti keren (They work hard)
mek mariben huden. (and they get beaten.)
Na maren, na maren ma (Don't beat me)
Bo man murdarena (But they kill me)
Hi man khere čhave, (I have children at home,)
Ko len likerala (Who will look after them?)

ITALY

Under Benito Mussolini Italy passed racial laws against Jews along similar lines to legislation enacted in Germany, but there seems to have been no central policy regarding Gypsies as a race. Three months after Italy's entry into the war (in June 1940), a circular was issued ordering the internment 'under vigorous surveillance' of nomadic Gypsies. Some family groups, concentrated first in staging camps, were transported to the islands surrounding Italy, and although their treatment by the police and soldiers was rough it was not often brutal. Many of the camps used were former barracks or monasteries, and, although these are often referred to in the literature as 'concentration camps', a better term, to distinguish their regimes from the camps in Germany and Poland which we describe in the next chapter, would be 'internment camps'.

Some Gypsies from Yugoslavia who had moved across the border into the zones of Gorizia and Udine before 1940 initially underwent internment in Abruzzi and then deportation to Sardinia or the Basilicata region in southern

Italy. Thulo Reinhardt remembers being deported as a child with his family to the Tremiti islands.

In 1938 a steamer brought one large party to forced exile in Sardinia. They were landed on the island and turned loose on the quayside without any provision being made for their maintenance. No camp was erected for their stay nor any guards set to watch over them. They were simply left to disperse inland and fend for themselves. Among the poorer villages of Sardinia the Gypsies received little help and few could follow their trades — smithing and horse-dealing — as a means of subsistence. Later an internment camp was opened at Perdasdefogu.

Others were detained in a camp in Puglia but many escaped the police nets and hid in the countryside, some later joining the partisans.

Gypsies who crossed later from Yugoslavia to escape the massacre carried out by the Ustashi in the fascist Croat state were sheltered by the Italian authorities. Detention in camps was partly for their own safety because they wanted to return to Yugoslavia to seek relatives and were in danger of falling into the hands of the Ustashi and Germans.

Among the camps set up for foreign Jews in 1940 after Italy had entered the war on the German side was Ferramonti di Tarsia in Cosenza province. The head of this camp, Paolo Salvatore, allowed the internees considerable freedom. In June 1943 the Gypsy families Philipoff and Kwik were brought to the camp. The Philipoffs held British passports. Both families remained there until the camp was freed by the allies in September 1943. More of the Kwiks then came to live in the camp premises, which remained open until 1945.

Not all Gypsies were so fortunate. The three families Bogdan, Gorman and Levak were held in Agnone in a special camp for Gypsies within a convent, where Zlato Levak's son died from malnutrition. Edvige Mayer died in Bozen/Gries concentration camp while Silvio Di Rocco and his family were imprisoned in Collefiorito camp because he had insulted the fascists.

In 1942 an existing camp at Tossicia (Teramo) was used for Gypsies who had been arrested in the Italian-occupied Trieste area of Yugoslavia. Some other Gypsies who ended up in Tossicia had of their own free will asked the Italian occupiers to send them out of Yugoslavia to Italy to escape from the Ustashi. The women were allowed out of the camp to beg for extra food from the local community.

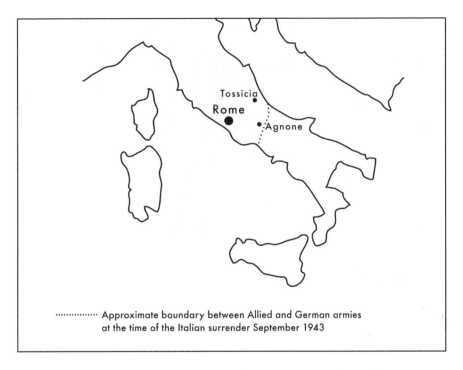

Approximate boundary between Allied and German armies
at the time of the Italian surrender September 1943

FIGURE 21. Map of Italy showing the area under German control in 1944

After the capitulation of Italy to the invading Allied troops on 8 September 1943 the Germans ordered the Italian police to organise the transport of the imprisoned Gypsies to Germany. However, the police opened the gates of Agnone and Tossicia camps and allowed the inmates to escape. Most of them fled to the mountains. The partisans told them which houses they could go to and the people were friendly to them. They brought them straw and the escapees slept there.

Much harder was the lot of Gypsy groups living in the region known as the Three Venices, which came under German military control after the Italian capitulation. They were rounded up, as in other German-occupied lands, to do forced labour in Germany or sent directly to the death camps. A proportion did not survive the long, cruel journey, packed into closed cattle trucks.

Partisans

Among the Gypsies who fought with the partisans were Amilcare Debar, in Piedmont, and Giuseppe Levakovitch, who was a member of the Osoppo

FIGURE 22. Amilcare Debar with another partisan on the mountain

Brigade in Friuli. The latter's wife Wilma was deported to Ravensbrück and from there to Dachau with two other women. Arcangelo Morelli was arrested under suspicion of helping the partisans and tortured in Aquila.

Some sacrificed their lives for the Allied cause, such as the partisan hero Walter Catter, who was hanged in Vicenza on 11 November 1944, and his cousin Giuseppe Catter, who died in action in the Ligurian mountains.

ROMANIA

In Romania there had always been an ambivalent attitude towards the large Gypsy minority. The Gypsies were admired as musicians and entertainers and were indispensable at weddings and celebrations, yet the majority had to live as distrusted social outcasts.

Once the fascist government of Ion Antonescu had established itself, after the abdication of King Carol in 1940, nationalistic feeling was strengthened.

Popular opinion was expressed by a Romanian captain who is quoted as saying, 'Mice, rats, crows, Gypsies, vagabonds and Jews don't need any documents.'[53]

The Romanian fascist paper *Eroica* said the Gypsy question was as important as that of the Jews. It bemoaned the 'prevailing dangerous opinion that the Gypsies form part of the Romanian race', as a result of which mixed marriages were increasing; the number of 'half-castes' had reached 600,000. *Eroica* demanded that such marriages be prohibited: 'Gypsies must be eliminated from any part they might play in the social life of the state.' The paper suggested all nomadic Gypsies should be placed in labour camps.

Racial scientists

Traian Herseni, in an article in the right-wing journal *Cuvintul nostrum* in January 1941, wanted to remove Jews, Gypsies and Greeks from Romanian soil. Dr Facaoru saw the Gypsies as a great danger for the Romanian people because of their large numbers, the fact that they were spread throughout the country, their increasing sedentarisation and the tolerance of the Romanians towards them. Like Himmler, he wanted to create a National Park where the traditional nomads could live. Dr Rulands proposed that, after deportation across the Dniester, they should be sterilised. Professor Ion Chelcea, in 1944, used quasi-scientific arguments and quotations from popular proverbs to uphold the biological and cultural inferiority of the Gypsies. He proposed the deportation of Gypsies from Romanian territory to preserve the biological and cultural riches of the Romanian nation. For the racial scientists the greatest danger came from the sedentary and assimilated Gypsies, as they might intermarry with Romanians and pollute their blood.

Transnistria

On 19 August 1941 Hitler confirmed that the Romanians were to occupy the conquered Ukraine as far as the river Bug. The following October Romania took Odessa, although most of the Crimea was taken over by the Germans. Romanian troops were responsible for security up to the river Dnieper and a new name was invented for the territory between the Dniester and Dnieper, Transnistria, which comprised some of the richest farmland of the USSR.

Some of this newly occupied area in the east was to be used as a dumping ground for Gypsies as the Germans had used Poland. The policy decided upon was a gradual clearing of Gypsies from the country rather than a mass deportation. To those to whom the policy was applied it brought disruption of family life, suffering, hardship, hunger and death, and the first to go would be the nomads.

The nomads' trail, 1942

The nomads were no danger to Romanian blood through intermarriage as they were isolated socially from the majority of society and had not been the prime target of the racial scientists. However, they had their own horses and wagons, which meant that no special transport was needed for their deportation; only guards were required to accompany them on the journey east.

In a few German-speaking villages in Transylvania the inhabitants resisted attempts to deport 'their' Gypsies. Clinic (Kelling) and Ungurei (Gergeschdorf) were among the villages where the Romanies remained unharmed. However, policemen on horseback forced the Gypsy chiefs from Profa, Tirgu Jiu and elsewhere to set off eastwards with their extended families. Mihai Tonu and Stanescu Zdrelea each led forty families. A few leaders set off willingly, not knowing what awaited them, and up to 13,000 nomads followed the trail towards the river Bug.

On arrival they had to build huts for themselves. Some dug holes to sleep in and broke up the wagons to use as a roof and protection against the weather. The rest of the wagon was gradually burnt up as fuel to keep warm and the horses were eaten. Conditions were hard that first winter. At night the temperature dropped and every morning there were frozen bodies to be found; it is said 1,500 died after one freezing night.

The nomads had been able to take their gold with them, and at night they would creep out of the camp to exchange gold for food in the neighbouring villages. Those who had no gold had to beg. Although they were surrounded by barbed wire, the camps were guarded ghettos rather than labour camps and for much of the time the inmates could leave not only to shop but also to celebrate weddings and baptisms in Russian Orthodox churches nearby.

Removal of sedentary Gypsies, September 1942

In eight days in September 1942 a further 13,000 Gypsies, including many sedentary from the Bucharest area, were transported across to the other side of the Dniester crammed into nine trains. General Constantin Vasiliu was in charge of this operation. Petre Radita has described the departure of one transport:

[The Gypsies were] despatched from Bucharest in cattle trucks with only the possessions they could hold, the journey took some weeks with stops and starts and because of the cold nights, lack of blankets and inadequate food supply many died of hunger and exposure before arriving at the river Bug in the Ukraine. Those that had survived were lodged in huts and later made to work digging trenches. Those found with gold teeth had them pulled out. Two children caught carrying messages to the partisans were executed in front of their parents.[54]

In 1942, as part of this policy of 'purification of the Romanian nation', the sedentary Gypsies of the wholly Gypsy village of Buda-Ursari (now in Moldova) were taken to a camp in the town of Nikolaev in the Ukraine. Many women and children died on the way. One man, Bogdan Nikulaje, lost all the members of his family. A secure camp was set up at Tiraspol in 1942 in which anyone caught returning from Transnistria to Romania was interned; the inmates worked in the surrounding fields.

The policy of transporting the Gypsies into the Ukraine aroused opposition among the local German officials. The Reichskommissar for the Ukraine wrote on the subject to the Minister for Occupied Eastern Territories in August 1942. After this a letter was sent from the Minister to the Foreign Office in Berlin, dated 11 September 1942, pointing out the danger that these Gypsies would try to settle on the east bank of the Bug and would then be a bad influence on the Ukrainian population. The Minister said the area set aside for Gypsies was in fact populated by ethnic Germans and asked the Foreign Office to persuade Romania to change its policy.[55] From 1943 the deportations ceased.

As far as we know, no further large-scale activity took place against the Romanian Gypsies after 1942 and those who had not been deported remained comparatively free. Some served in the army. Pirvan Regalie, from the village of Clejani near Bucharest, fought at Stalingrad.

Returning home

Towards the end of 1943, after the Germans had been driven back over the Bug with their Romanian allies, the gates of the large camp at Tiraspol were opened and Gypsies took the opportunity to try to return to Romania. Weakened by months of hunger and cold, many children and old people did not survive this return journey. The survivors eventually reached Dabuleni, Profa, Tirgu Jiu and other towns from which they had been driven out.

After the war, when the Romanian People's Court appointed an investigation committee to look into war crimes, it took an unfavourable view of the living conditions of the deportees:

> Tens of thousands of defenceless Gypsies were herded together in Transnistria. Over half were struck by typhus. The civilian police practised unprecedented terror; everyone's life was uncertain; tortures were cruel. The commanders lived in debauchery with beautiful Gypsy women and maintained personal harems. Approximately 36,000 Gypsies fell victim to Antonescu's fascist regime.

The figure of 36,000 for 'victims' is too high. The various accounts which have been found since the archives were opened suggest that some 13,000 Gypsies were deported to the east by train. A similar number of nomads had gone to Transnistria with their wagons, making a total of 26,000. It is estimated that from the total of deportees some 20,000 perished in the east.

Antonescu said at his trial that the Gypsies had been deported because they had robbed people during the curfew and because the Governor of Transnistria needed workers. He and Vasiliu were executed for war crimes.

SLOVAKIA

The treatment of the many Gypsies within the puppet fascist state of Slovakia, although hard, did not reach the level of the systematic extermination practised in the German-occupied regions of Czechoslovakia (Bohemia and Moravia). For this reason it was considered a place of refuge by Gypsies from other areas, although the Slovak fascist leader Alexandr Mach, addressing the Hitler Youth in May 1942, promised that the solution of the Gypsy problem would follow after that of the Jews.

From 1940 Gypsies in many towns were forbidden to enter parks, cafés and restaurants or to use public transport. In 1941 local authorities received instructions from the Ministry of the Interior to expel Gypsies from the quarters they occupied in nearly every town and village in Slovakia. As with many fascist decrees, the orders were executed differently from one place to another and there was very little displacement until the expulsion order was reissued in 1943.

From 1941 compulsory labour was imposed upon Jews and Gypsies. Again, the effect of the order varied from town to town. At the village of

FIGURE 23. Work brigade in Slovakia

Smizany the Gypsy community of 500 had become well integrated and here no one was sent to perform forced labour. At Letanovce the mayor tried to protect the Gypsies but the Hlinka Guards (Slovak fascist police) ordered him to send Gypsies to the forced labour camps. However, he selected only two, both men with alleged bad reputations for drinking and anti-social behaviour. They worked at a railway construction camp near Presov, survived the war and returned to the village afterwards. Again, in the settlement of Rakusy the Gypsies were left alone until 1944 when Gypsies and Slovaks had to dig trenches against the advancing Red Army.

Work-camps for Gypsies existed in many places, including Dubnica, Hanusovce and Ilava. A Gypsy from Janova relates how, towards the end of the war, he was sent to dig trenches for four months, after which he was transferred to a camp in Poland. They received very little to eat and the bread was so thin that 'you could see the whole length and breadth of the country through it'.

The Ministry of the Interior wrote to district offices in July 1943 pointing out that they had not all complied with earlier laws on the evacuation of Gypsies from towns and villages. All Gypsies had to be shifted to places well away from roads and execution was to be the punishment for any refusing to move.

In 1944 pressure on the Gypsies increased. A law in June accused the Gypsies of spreading typhoid through the country and effectively banned them from using the state railways. In order to travel they first had to get a doctor's certificate that they were clean and free from typhoid, then this certificate had to be presented to the district office to obtain a travel permit. The travel permit was valid only for the outward journey and the whole procedure had to be gone through again for the return.

Resistance

The Gypsies actively supported the National Uprising against the puppet government in the summer of 1944. As a result, when the fascist regime called in German troops and the uprising was brutally suppressed, the Gypsies were to suffer.

Among Gypsy partisan officers was Tomas Farkas, who led a mixed group of Gypsies and Slovaks. His unit held up the German counter-attack in a gorge near Tisovec, some seventy-five kilometres east of Banska Bystrica, the centre of the rebellion. As the Germans pressed forward the unit had to retreat to the mountains. In consequence, Tomas Farkas's family was punished and his son was sent to a concentration camp. Fortunately, he survived the war. Tomas Farkas and Anton Facuna, who was dropped in by parachute to act as a liaison officer between the partisans and the US military mission, were both decorated after the war.

Pogroms

A large number of pogroms were carried out by local fascists as they took revenge after the suppression of the National Uprising. All but two of a community of 111 men, women and children were killed at Ilija. At Kriz nad Hronom the Gypsies were locked in a hut which was then set on fire. Those attempting to escape from the burning building were shot. Murders took place at many other locations. In the village of Cierny Balog over fifty Gypsies met a similar death in two huts, after being forced to carry the cans of petrol themselves. Later other Gypsies had to dig a collective grave for the dead. A massacre in Nerenica left only two families alive.

Earlier in the war the Gypsies of Tisovec had been forced out of the village and had set up camp in the woods. The men joined the partisans but when their group had to move to another area the unit commander left heavy weapons and machine guns hidden near the Gypsy camp. After the Germans had reoccupied the area an intelligence officer who spoke Russian was sent there disguised as a Russian partisan. After making some of the Gypsies drunk with vodka, he asked them how many weapons they had. They began to boast about the machine guns. Shortly afterwards, the Hlinka Guards surrounded the settlement and shot the men in front of their families and then killed the women and children. The bodies were thrown into a lime quarry. Only one girl survived. The victims of this massacre are commemorated in a memorial at Banska Bystrica.

The fascists suspected the Gypsies of another village, Slatina, of giving food to the partisans. On 23 November 1944, they killed all fifty-nine persons they found in the camp; only three members of the community survived. In the same month 747 persons, mainly Gypsy men, were shot at Kremenicka and buried in a mass grave. Near Nemecka Gypsies and others were shot. Their bodies were burnt and the ashes thrown into the river Hron.

It is generally accepted that only the end of the war saved the Gypsies of Slovakia from sharing the fate of their fellows in Bohemia and Moravia. One writer has mentioned that accusations of cannibalism were made against the Gypsies as part of the preparation for a campaign against them but, in the event, only a few hundred of the wartime Gypsy population of Slovakia, estimated at over 100,000, died at the hands of the fascists.

The aftermath

The order for the expulsion of the Gypsies from communities in Slovakia where they were already largely sedentary, accepted and integrated had an effect which is still being felt today. Forced to leave their houses and make primitive camps for themselves in woods and scrubland usually several kilometres away, they existed for several years as outcasts, the children denied education and the parents barely able to scrape together the necessities of life. The Gypsies of Slovakia for the most part still live in isolated ghettos today.

7

CONCENTRATION CAMPS AND MEDICAL EXPERIMENTS

Few concentration camps did not have their share of Gypsy prisoners. We deal first with the early labour camps in Germany which later became 'international' concentration camps, then with Auschwitz and finally with the extermination camps. The dates of opening are given.

DACHAU (OPENED IN 1933)

One of the early concentration camps, Dachau, was among the first to hold Gypsies — a small number who were shut up there on the grounds that they constituted an asocial element. In 1936 Joseph Kramer, who worked in the camp office that same year, said that at that time there were 'only political prisoners, criminals, beggars and Gypsies in the camp'. The guards had orders to shoot if any prisoners attempted to escape.

After 1939 prisoners were brought from the Austrian Burgenland and other parts of Europe. Arpad Krok recounts that he was arrested at the age of twelve in the Hungarian-occupied part of Slovakia and, after a period in a Hungarian camp, he was sent to Dachau. There he contracted typhus and was thrown on to a pile of dead bodies, but an SS woman doctor saved him and gave him food. As a result he survived and was still in Dachau when it was liberated by the Americans.

SACHSENHAUSEN (1936)

In 1938 German Gypsies were sent to Sachsenhausen as 'work-shy'. As prisoners came in later from the occupied countries the Gypsies formed a community apart. A prisoner recounts:

> When it was a question of standing in a queue in front of the clinic, Norwegians, Dutch and Germans always had to stand in front. Then there were the middle classes, from Frenchmen and Belgians down to Ukrainians. Right at the bottom came Jews and Gypsies.

A Norwegian inmate of Sachsenhausen described the arrival of Gypsy children from Ravensbrück on 4 March 1945:

FIGURE 24. Gypsy prisoners in a concentration camp

> The children from Ravensbrück were Gypsy children, fantastically beautiful and charming, hungry and musical. A group of them were given food in Norwegian Block 16 and gave a concert in gratitude.[56]

BUCHENWALD (1937)

Not all Gypsies entering Buchenwald were registered as such although there were special barracks allocated to Gypsies. This makes it impossible to give an accurate figure for the number that came there, died there or went on to other camps. Certainly there were several thousand. As early as June 1938 some 600 Gypsy men and boys from Germany were imprisoned in Buchenwald. Even before the war, life in the camp was strict and brutal, and the penalty for trying to escape was death.

At the end of 1938, on the orders of Major Rodl, Deputy Camp Commander, a band was formed — one of many such bands in camps. Most of the musicians were Gypsies. At first they played guitars and harmonicas, and then a trombone, and later a drum and trumpet, were added. The prisoners had to pay for these instruments themselves and worked by day in the lumber-yard or carpenter's shop, rehearsing only after work. One prisoner, Eugen Kogon, recounted:

> It was ghastly to see and hear how the Gypsies played their lively marches while the mistreated prisoners carried their dead or dying comrades past the band into the camp, or how the musicians had to play during the counting of blows while prisoners were being beaten . . . But then I remember New Year's Eve 1939. Suddenly the sound of a Gypsy violin drifted out from one of the barracks far off, as though from happier times and climes — tunes from the Hungarian steppe, melodies from Vienna and Budapest, songs from home.[57]

In the winter of 1938/9 several hundred Gypsies died because of the bad conditions, lack of clothing and blankets, poor food and over-work. They were meant to die.

During 1942 at least three transports with over 200 Gypsy prisoners went from Buchenwald to the Auschwitz main camp. By 1944 few Gypsies remained in Buchenwald and these were mostly from Germany, with a few from Poland and Bohemia; they lived in Block 47 alongside prisoners classified as asocials. Like them, they wore black triangle badges. Gypsies still had places in the band and one looked after the bear in the camp zoo.

Then in April 1944 Gypsies began to arrive from Auschwitz, where the special Gypsy camp was already being disbanded. Initially put into the 'Little Camp' (quarantine quarters), some moved illegally from there into the main camp and others were transferred officially. These Gypsy inmates had at first to sleep in the open air and beg food from better-off French inmates.

Over 2,000 Gypsies arrived in two large transports. Many had to be moved to Dora, an overflow camp for Buchenwald, and were to die there. The younger ones were later returned to Auschwitz for extermination. Again, Kogon describes the scene.

> Even hardened prisoners were deeply moved when the SS in the autumn of 1944 singled out and herded together all Jewish and Gypsy youngsters. The screaming, sobbing children, frantically trying to get to their fathers or protectors among the prisoners, were surrounded by a wall of carbines and machine pistols and taken away to be sent to Auschwitz for gassing.

The Gypsies at Buchenwald at this time came from widely separated parts of Europe, including Bohemia, Carpathia, Croatia, northern and eastern France, southern Poland and Ruthenia. Some Gypsies were still there in the last days of the camp. Three women were on the list of deaths for January 1945. In February 200 men went to Dora and then on to Bergen-Belsen. Not more than forty of them survived. One prisoner wrote that he met no Gypsies when he returned to Buchenwald in March 1945, while other witnesses say there were a few.

MAUTHAUSEN (1938)

The Nazis tried to destroy the official records of Mauthausen but some lists of prisoners have survived. These contain the names of Gypsies, who were generally accommodated in Block 6. In July 1941 a transport of ninety-one Gypsies was sent from Buchenwald to Mauthausen, of whom one at least, Robert Schneeberger, survived. The records for February 1945 state that ten Gypsies died in the camp that month. A Gypsy woman chosen as an overseer was, when her race was discovered, transferred to Auschwitz.

RAVENSBRÜCK (1939)

The first large party of Gypsies to come to Ravensbrück concentration camp arrived on 19 June 1939 from the Austrian Burgenland, not long after the camp first opened. Women holding their small children close had to remain sitting on the ground for two days while the process of admission went on.

From time to time other groups of children were placed in the camp, many in the period 1942–3 being of Polish nationality. Some were separated from their parents and relatives and dispersed through the barracks, while other children were allowed to remain with a parent.

The Gypsies wore black triangles, like the so-called asocials, but formed a separate group. At first they were all housed in Block 22, where conditions were the worst in the camp. Starvation compelled them to beg outside the barracks of the Norwegian prisoners, who received food parcels. Gypsy women worked in the clothes factory and two little girls, aged nine or ten, were working in the masseur and hairdressing salon early in 1942.

Selections and mass killings appear to have begun late in 1943. Erdely Kapoline (no. 35726) was among a group gassed, probably in autumn 1944. Mass executions took place during February 1945 and 1,356 Gypsies appear on the list of those murdered. In addition, Gypsies were sterilised at Ravensbrück (information about this is given below).

AUSCHWITZ (1940)

Later camps such as Auschwitz were run as concentration camps from the beginning. Gypsies were among the prisoners in the main camp here. At least two transports of Czech Gypsies arrived during 1942, and during the week ending 18 October seventeen died. It is thought that a group of ninety-two Gypsies who arrived in December 1942 were gassed on arrival. Gypsies arriving at Auschwitz in January the following year were placed in Block 18 and later transferred to a new camp.

Himmler made a visit in 1941 and ordered the construction of a second camp, Birkenau, near Auschwitz; this was large enough to hold 200,000 persons. Even after the establishment of the special compound at Birkenau, some Gypsies still stayed in the old camp: on 20 January 1944, 479 remained

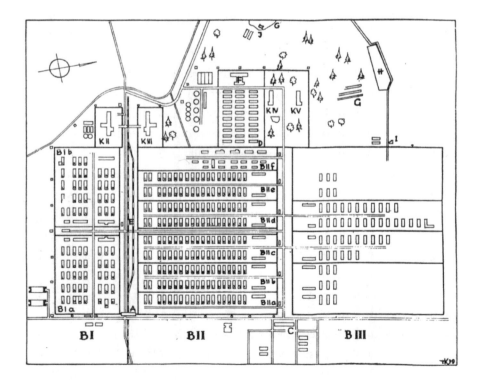

FIGURE 25. Plan of Auschwitz

on the list. During that year some Gypsies who were fit for work were transferred from Birkenau back to the old Auschwitz camp prior to the liquidation of the Gypsy camp, although some managed to return clandestinely to
Birkenau to join their families.

Auschwitzate hi kher baro
(a song composed by an unknown prisoner in Auschwitz)

Auschwitzate hi kher baro. (In Auschwitz there is a big hut.)
Odoi bešel mro pirano, (There sits my sweetheart,)
bešel, bešel, gondinel (he sits, sits and thinks)
the pre mande pobisterel. (and forgets about me.)
Auschwitzate bokha bare (In Auschwitz there is great hunger)
the so te hal amen nane, (and we have nothing to eat,)
ani koda kotor maro (not even a piece of bread)
O blokaris bi-bahtalo. (The block leader is harsh.)

The Gypsy camp at Auschwitz-Birkenau[58]

A section of Birkenau was set aside for Gypsies and from February 1943 they
came in from all over Europe. Designed to hold 10,000 prisoners, the section was completely full. The thirty long stables used as dormitories should
have housed 300 each but at times some of them had over twice this number
crammed into them. Unusually, this was a so-called 'family camp' with women
and children in some of the barracks while the men were held in others.

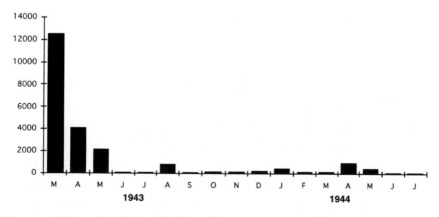

FIGURE 26. Rate of arrivals at the Gypsy Camp

Contrary to clauses in Himmler's Auschwitz Order, many assimilated and ex-service Gypsies soon showed up there among the prisoners. Camp Commandant Rudolf Höss wrote later:

> Persons were arrested who could not possibly be regarded as belonging to the category that it was intended to intern. Many men were arrested while on leave from the front, despite high decorations and several wounds, simply because their father or mother or grandfather had been a Gypsy or part-Gypsy. Even a very senior Party member whose Gypsy grandfather had settled in Leipzig was among them. He himself had a large business there and had been decorated more than once during the First World War. Another was a girl student who had been a leader in the Berlin League of German Girls. There were many more such cases.[59]

We cannot believe it was merely intended to intern Gypsies in Auschwitz until after the war and then release them, as Höss was to suggest. Since even the privileged Rom Gypsies, exempted in theory from the Auschwitz order, faced sterilisation outside the camps, it is clear that the mainly Sinti Gypsies in Auschwitz would not be allowed to procreate. Possibly they were to be kept at Auschwitz and used for various experimental purposes until they died out. The whole family camp was perhaps an attempt to see what could be done with other non-Aryan races the Nazis would have met if German expansion had been continued.

Höss in his prison diary describes a later visit by Himmler:

> In July 1943 [sic] Himmler visited the camp. He made a most thorough inspection of everything in the Gypsy Camp noting the overcrowded barrack huts, the unhygienic conditions, the crammed hospital building . . . He noted the mortality rate, which was relatively low in comparison with that of the camp as a whole . . . He saw it all in detail and as it really was and he ordered me to destroy them. Those capable of work were first to be separated from the others as with the Jews. I pointed out to him that the personnel of the Gypsy Camp was not precisely what he envisaged being sent to Auschwitz. He thereupon ordered that the Central Police Headquarters should carry out a sorting as quickly as possible. This in fact took one year. The Gypsies capable of work were transferred to another camp. About 4,000 Gypsies were left by August 1944 and these had to go into the gas chamber. [The visit was in fact in 1942]

FIGURE 27. Portrait of a Gypsy woman in Auschwitz drawn by a Jewish prisoner, Dina Babbitt

The sorting-out process — if this was true — should have been of those exempted from Himmler's original order and their families, not of those suitable for forced labour in other concentration camps. Höss, however, said:

> I made a report to the Police Headquarters. As a result the Gypsy camp was constantly under examination and many releases took place. But these were scarcely noticeable, so great was the number of those who remained.

SS officer Pery Broad, however, gives a contrary view:

> From the camp some letters were sent to the Central Gypsy Office asking for certain cases [settled and educated Gypsies] to be released but these were all refused. The police refused to release anyone from Auschwitz. The Central Office knew it was Hitler's aim to wipe out all the Gypsies

without exception and the exemptions in the Auschwitz order were only a blind. [They] wrote to Auschwitz asking them not to send any more requests to release Gypsies.

We will now look at the general conditions in the camp, as interpreted from reports by survivors:

> In the Gypsy camp there were large barracks that had a hole in the front and rear. Those were the doors. On single planks in large wooden boxes lay five to six persons. The sanitation was catastrophic. There was no paint on the walls. The water facilities were as good as non-existent . . . The hygienic conditions were indescribable . . . It was a bog with horse stables without windows. The people waded up to their ankles in slime.

On arrival the Gypsies were tattooed with a camp number. Their heads were shaved but the hair allowed to grow again. They received no special clothing but in the early period they wore a black triangle, as asocials. Possessions, including jewellery, were taken from them. The families were not separated, but the guards tried to control in which barrack people slept. A sick barrack, a quarantine barrack and also a special barrack for sick children existed, though in fact these were no different from any other.

Some were made to work from the beginning. Elisabeth Guttenberger wrote that fourteen days after her arrival she was allotted to a labour commando. She had to carry stones. Between April and June 1943 the Gypsies did some canalisation work and a work commando cut trees in the forests. For an unknown reason, the majority were not allocated any work and this gave other prisoners the impression that the Gypsies were excused forced labour.

Food in the Gypsy camp was totally inadequate:

> The Gypsies were all undernourished. I controlled and tasted the food in the kitchen. It was a sort of grain soup, no, rather it was a water soup with a few grains swimming in it.

Dr Franz Lucas, a Nazi doctor based at Ravensbrück, who visited briefly the Auschwitz Gypsy camp, claimed at a post-war trial that he tried to improve the food:

> The imprisoned Gypsies were often shrunken to skeletons. I went to the kitchen and found that the food did not contain the prescribed 1,680

calories. I wrote a memo immediately but Hartjenstein [Commander of the whole camp 1943–4] said, 'Oh, they are only Gypsies after all.'

Elisabeth Guttenberger said that at first she received parcels from outside, but after these were stopped, her mother, sister, father and brothers died of starvation. We cite Höss again:

> It was quite impossible to provide proper food for the children . . . The Food Ministry laid down that no special children's food might be issued to the Concentration Camps.

As a result of the poor food and unhygienic conditions, disease was rife in the camp. From May 1943 typhus raged, along with scurvy, diarrhoea and water canker (or noma). Six hundred were sick with smallpox that month and 1,000 the same summer. Others suffered from a form of chicken-pox (*varicella variolo formis*) which resembled smallpox. We know that several hundreds died from these diseases.

Lucie Adelsberger, a prisoner who worked as a nurse in the Gypsy camp, described the minimal hospital facilities. The sick barracks, like the other buildings, had previously been stables. They had no windows but some small covered openings in the roof for light and there were holes in the walls and ceiling. Inside, each side was lined by three-storey wooden bunks strewn with straw sacks and thin blankets. In the middle stood two wooden tables used as a couch for examining patients, and a stove. Ten persons slept in places designed for four, while water dripped from the roof on to the bunks. On the bottom row patients who could not move lay in their own dirt. Most of the nurses were untrained Gypsies whose job was to measure temperatures and give out food. The doctors' main task was to keep a check on the numbers of dead and make sure they tallied. For medicines the staff had two ampoules of camphor and a bottle of digitalis each week, plus sacks of kaolin, a treatment for diarrhoea. Every day twenty to thirty died and their bodies were placed in one corner of the barrack and collected each evening by a special commando.

Dr Josef Mengele set up an experimental barrack in the Gypsy camp. Here research was done on twin births, dwarfs and giants and also on gangrene of the face (another term for noma, or water canker). Non-Gypsy twins were also brought to him here. When the final gassing of Gypsies took place, the bodies of twelve sets of twins were saved from burning in the crematorium for autopsies. Dr Mengele had marked ZS on their chests with his special chalk before they went to the gas chamber. Both Dr Bendel and Dr Epstein, prisoners employed by Mengele for these experiments, said he judged these more important than attending to the sick Gypsies.

Most Gypsies had come in families and a high proportion of children lived in the camp. The orphans were kept separately in Blocks 22 and 23. There was a children's playground between the wash-room and the kindergarten, with a roundabout and other apparatus. Höss described it as 'a large playground where the children could run about to their hearts' content and play with toys of every description'. The purpose was propaganda. The special playground displayed a large notice, 'Children's School'. On occasions the children were driven into the playground and photographed.

Hermann Langbein, a prisoner, describes the barrack where the mothers who had given birth lay:

> The only anxiety the SS took was to see that the newly born had their prisoner number tattooed immediately on the upper thigh. There was no special food, hardly any water. The floor was of clay and at one end there was a curtain. There I saw a pile of children's bodies and, among them, rats.

Of course, the child mortality rate was extraordinarily high and not many new-born babies survived more than a few weeks, as some examples taken from the official records show:

GIRLS	BORN	DIED
Z.8893	14 June 1943	25 June 1943
Z.8894	14 June 1943	7 July 1943
Z.8895	11 June 1943	3 July 1943
Z.8896	12 June 1943	17 July 1943
Z.8897	14 June 1943	17 June 1943

Apart from killing by neglect, there was deliberate cruelty and murder in the Auschwitz Gypsy Camp, in spite of higher instruction to treat the Gypsies differently from Jews. Morning roll-call lasted from 6 to 8 A.M., and sometimes all day. Often during the roll-call 'Sport' was called and the weakened prisoners had to do exercises while Franz Hofmann, Camp Commander for part of 1943, hit many of them. In midsummer 1943 all room

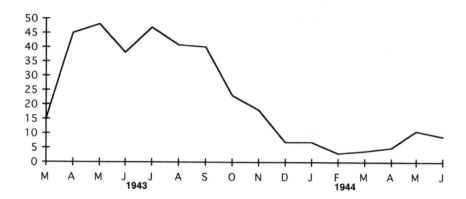

FIGURE 28. Recorded births in the Gypsy Camp

orderlies and barrack secretaries had to do Sport. Then they had to sing *Das kann doch einen Seemann nicht erschüttern* ('That can't worry a sailor') and then do Sport again. During the second Sport seven or eight people died.

There was little relief from the hard life in Auschwitz. Eighty-two Gypsies are known to have been imprisoned in an underground cell during 1943 for various offences against the Auschwitz rules. Once a month everyone had to go through the sauna for delousing at a temperature of 50–60°C, during which process several Gypsies suffered heart attacks and some died. After morning roll-call those not joining work commandos were left alone for the rest of the day to walk up and down the 'main street' between the barracks or to sit outside them until the evening curfew. Höss wrote:

> If one went into their camp they would often run out of the barracks to play their musical instrument or to let their children dance or perform their usual tricks.

Broad set up an orchestra in the Gypsy camp and once a full-scale concert was arranged. But this was interrupted by a curfew during which the SS came to fetch many hundreds of Gypsies to be gassed. Later all instruments were taken away, and this loss spelt the end of an interest in life for many. The SS men sometimes came in the evenings and took young women off to dance in their barracks.

Attempted escapes

Many prisoners tried to escape from Auschwitz although they knew well the fate that awaited them if recaptured. As the entries in the secretly kept diary *Auschwitz-Hefte* laconically put it:

> On 4 May 1943, Jozef Cerinek (Z.1904) and Franz Rozycka (Z.2035) tried to escape from a work commando. They were put in Block II bunker and shot on 22 May.

Soon after the erection of the barracks, the Gypsy camp was completed by an electrified wire fence and a watch-post built at the gate. These measures did not deter Gypsies from trying to break out and by August 1943 around eighty had been shot after recapture, torture and detention in the notorious Bunker in Block II.

At the end of 1943, after Höss left Auschwitz, the camp authorities did not treat those recaptured so harshly. Three caught escaping in November and December were merely locked up, as were some non-Gypsies recaptured about the same time. There was an attempted mass break-out on 1 February 1944, when at least three Gypsies were shot as they tried to flee from a Punishment Company which was working in the forest.

We know of one successful escaper, Vincenc Daniel, who fled not once but twice. He had been arrested as a nomad in occupied Slovakia as early as April 1942 and sent to the main camp in Auschwitz. Here he was given the number 33804. He escaped from a working party at the Buna Works and managed to return to Moravia. He hid in the area of Velika Bitres but was caught stealing food and sentenced to six months in prison. Bad luck meant that he was still in jail when the order came for all Gypsy prisoners to be sent to the special camp in Auschwitz. He was included in a transport that left Brno on 21 August 1943. He made his second escape while the prisoners were being deloused and once more returned to the Czech lands where, helped by Czechs, he hid in the woods till the end of the war.

Massacres

Before the final liquidation of the camp, two massacres took place. In March 1943, 1,700 Polish Gypsies arrived from Bialystok. They received no numbers and were isolated in Blocks 20 and 22. A few days later during an evening curfew they were all gassed 'as suspected typhus cases'. They may have been killed because the SS thought that if Polish Gypsies fled the camp they could more easily hide than other escapers.

Then, on 25 May 1943, 1,042 Gypsies were dragged out of various blocks and gassed. The SS came to each barrack, including the sick bay, and looked for the numbers they had on a list, as these people had already been dispersed among the different barracks. They comprised passengers on two transports which had arrived on 12 May from Bialystok and Austria. Suspected typhus may well have been the main reason for the second of these mass killings.

A frustrated massacre

On 16 May 1943 a curfew was ordered. In the evening lorry-loads of SS men arrived. They surrounded the barracks and went inside to get the Gypsies out. The Gypsies had been warned that the announcement of a curfew would mean that the time for their murder had arrived. They had armed themselves with knives, spades, crowbars and stones and refused to leave their barracks. The SS men went to the office of the Block leaders to discuss what to do. A few minutes later a whistle was heard. All the SS men got into the lorries and drove off. The curfew was lifted.[60]

The respite was not to be for long, though. More of the young inmates were to be moved from the camp.

Transports out

If we are to believe Camp Commander Höss, it was two months after this attempted massacre that Himmler decided — in July 1943 — that the Gypsy Camp must eventually be done away with.

As the date for the liquidation of the camp approached, healthy young Gypsies were selected so they could go to work in other concentration camps and to remove anyone capable of serious resistance.

On 23 May 1944 more than 1,500 Gypsy prisoners were sent to the main camp at Auschwitz. Two hundred were then transported to Flossenburg and Ravensbrück.

The remainder were held until 2 August when they were loaded onto a train which stopped at Birkenau in a unique event so that relations in the Gypsy camp could say goodbye. The story was that they were going to Hindenberg to build a new camp for everyone. In fact, the destination of the prisoners on the train was Buchenwald and their relations left behind in the camp were to be gassed that very night.

The liquidation of the Gypsy Camp

The last males entered in the record book are for 8 July 1944, and the last females 21 July. The order had clearly gone out that no more Gypsies were to be sent to Auschwitz. From 28 July extra food was allocated to the children's barracks. The day now drew near for the end of the Gypsy Camp.

After the departure of the final transport, referred to above, a strict curfew was imposed. Some 2,800 women, children and old men were left in the Gypsy Camp. The lorries arrived at 8 P.M. with SS men led by Captain Clausen. Some Gypsies guessed what was in store for them but the Germans tried to allay suspicions. Everyone was given a ration of bread and salami as they came out of their quarters and some believed at first that they must be going to another camp. The lorries were driven off in another direction and only when darkness had fallen did they then turn towards the gas chambers. During the transfer the majority of Gypsies resisted as best they could, and the final liquidation has been described by several internees from adjacent sections of Birkenau:

> We were within easy earshot of the terrible final scenes as German criminal prisoners using clubs and dogs were let loose in the camp against the women, children and old men. A desperate cry from a young Czech-speaking lad suddenly rent the air. Please, Mr SS man, let me live. Blows with a club were the only answer.

> Terrible scenes took place. Women and children were on their knees in front of Mengele and Wilhelm Boger crying, 'Take pity, take pity on us'. Nothing helped. They were beaten down brutally, trampled on and pushed on to the trucks. It was a terrible, gruesome night. Some persons lay lifeless after being beaten and were also thrown on to the lorries. Lorries came to the orphans' block about 10.30 and to the isolation or hospital block at about 11 P.M. The SS and four prisoners lifted all the sick people out and also twenty-five healthy women who had been isolated with their children.

The reports by eyewitnesses show how, even though the active adults had been removed, the Gypsies struggled to the last. One woman threw herself on to an SS man, clawing him with her bare hands. Another woman hid during the action but she was found and gassed four days later. Four Gypsies had earlier been transferred to the Punishment Company and were overlooked when the Gypsy Camp was liquidated. They realised that they would be gassed. They begged everyone they thought had some influence to aid them. When they asked SS officer Emil Bednarek for help he hit them. Some time later these Gypsies were taken to the gas chamber.

After this gassing the bodies were put in ditches and burnt, as the crematorium was not working. Thus ended the sixteen-month life of the Gypsy Camp at Auschwitz.

Another SS officer, Boger, was sentenced in 1965 to life imprisonment for his activities in the camp but not those relating to the liquidation of the Gypsies, as these charges could not be proved. Broad was to be sentenced at the same trial to four years in prison for his part in selecting Jewish victims in the camp.

Statistics of Auschwitz

Some statistics of the Gypsy Camp have been discovered, including entries in the official register:

	No.
Males registered	10,094
Females registered	10,839
Total	20,933

The highest female number in the register was Z.10,849 but no names are entered against ten numbers and they were possibly not used (10,814 and 10,819–27). Some inmates were tattooed with higher numbers but were not entered in the register. Excluding some 360 children born in the camp who lived long enough to be given numbers, the total number of recorded admissions was around 20,600. This is by no means the total number of Gypsies brought to Auschwitz but simply those registered in the special Gypsy Camp.

Round figures for the fate of registered prisoners in the Gypsy camp are set out below:

Prisoners' fate	No.
Transported out	3,800
Killed	4,000*
Died in the camp	12,800

*1,000 on 25 May 1943, 3,000 on liquidation, 1944

To these figures must be added 1,700 gassed soon after arrival in March 1943 and not given numbers. Those who died (rather than being deliberately killed) did so because of inadequate food, the unhygienic conditions and lack of medical treatment; and some of the prisoners who were transported out before the liquidation were later brought back to Auschwitz and gassed.

Survivors fall into two categories: a small number of workers in the camp office who were not included in the liquidation and those who were transported to other camps and managed to remain alive there until the end of the war. They included Max Friedrich (Z.2894), Elisabeth Guttenberger (Z.2987) and Hillie Weiss (Z.4609), all to be witnesses at the Auschwitz trial. Out of more than 20,000, only a few hundred lived through their experiences.

Few Gypsies were left in the main Auschwitz camp. A roll-call there on 17 January 1945 — the day the SS began to evacuate the camp — showed four male Gypsies. There may have been some women, plus a few registered under other nationalities. There was just one Gypsy among the 4,000 ill persons left when the survivors were counted after their liberation by Soviet troops on 27 January.

OTHER CAMPS

Several thousand Gypsies were interned at Bergen-Belsen, which had become a concentration camp in 1944. Here again there was a Gypsy orchestra which, it is said, went from hut to hut both day and night collecting money and food. Food, water and medical care were in short supply.[61] Survivors included one Gypsy woman, deported from Hungary first to Dachau and then to Bergen-Belsen.

The first mention of Gypsies in Maidenek (Lublin) we have found is in the account of a young man who was taken there in 1940. In June 1942 the Senior Prisoner was a Gypsy named Galbavy from Holič. Hanna Brzezinska

Figure 29. Map showing the main concentration and extermination camps in Germany and Poland

came there from Rechlin at the end of 1944 or early 1945. She met Gypsies from Czechoslovakia, Germany and Poland in the camp, all of them slowly starving to death.

No complete picture has come to light concerning Neuengamme but there are several references to Gypsies being held there. Gypsy internees had to wear brown triangles, while the asocials carried brown and black badges. Though called 'Zintys' by the other prisoners, they may not have all been Sinti Gypsies. There were also small Gypsy children, some born in a concentration camp and many of them orphans. They kept the parade ground and streets clean, starting work as soon as the other prisoners left the camp in the morning.

Other concentration camps at which the presence of Gypsies is attested included Belzec, Deutmergen, Gross-Rosen, Gusen, Natzweiler, Niederhagen, Rechlin, Sobibor, Stutthof, Theresienstadt and Zwodau.

LODZ GHETTO

As part of the plan to empty Germany and Austria of Gypsies, it was decided by Heydrich to use part of the Jewish ghetto at Lodz (Poland). A consignment of 5,000 persons was to be sent there. Eichmann visited the ghetto and claimed at his trial that he sent the Gypsies to Lodz to save their lives.

The first transports came in October 1941 and by the middle of November the whole intended number had arrived. The 5,000 included over 2,600 children from Austria and other countries. The senior Jewish ghetto representative, Chaim Rumkowski, was ordered to make room for the Gypsies, and Jewish occupants had to vacate the houses in one quarter. This was then surrounded by a double and in some places a triple wall of barbed wire and an excavated ditch filled with water.

In this small sectioned-off area the Gypsies were again interned in their family groups. During the day cries and lamentations filled the air and every evening the Jews saw cars full of German soldiers going in the direction of the Gypsy quarter. That bitterly cold winter the soldiers smashed all the windows of the houses. Two weeks later a typhus epidemic broke out. The Germans gave no medical aid whatever, but Jewish doctors volunteered to go in and help; at least one of them, Dr Glaser, died of the disease. During the first two months 613 people perished. Each day carts loaded with bodies had to be taken from the quarter. Some of the corpses showed signs of beatings. Others had rope tied around their necks.

A group of 120 adults was taken from the ghetto to work in a German factory and a small number of these were to survive until the liberation. Then, early in 1942, the remaining Gypsies were taken in lorries from Lodz to Chelmno and gassed there.

EXTERMINATION CAMPS

As well as the concentration camps, where inmates were worked or starved to death, the Nazis built other camps where all the prisoners were killed on arrival. In July 1941 Hermann Göring (Hitler's deputy at the time) talked to Heydrich and the latter began to set up these death camps — Belzec, Chelmno, Sobibor and Treblinka. The four camps were in addition to extermination centres set up at Auschwitz and Maidenek. The aim was the extermination of east European Jewry, but the opportunity was also taken to murder those Gypsies living in areas near the camps.

Chelmno

The Polish War Crimes Commission reported that 5,000 Gypsies were murdered at Chelmno, but full details have not been uncovered and estimates vary. Another source puts the figure at 15,000 out of 1,300,000 people exterminated there. These included the several thousand Gypsies who came from Lodz when the city's ghetto was liquidated. Others were brought from elsewhere in Poland. The Germans used poison gas and machine guns to dispatch some groups.

Treblinka

No total figures are available for Treblinka nor can any estimate be made of the total number of Gypsies murdered there. Most of the prisoners who helped to dispose of the dead were themselves later killed. There is very little documentation for any of the extermination camps.[62]

> A number of Bessarabian Gypsies appeared [it is not known whether they had been sent by the German or Romanian authorities]. Two hundred men and eight hundred women and children. The Gypsies came on foot. Behind them came their wagons drawn by horses. Afterwards they were made to undress for 'baths' and then driven by guard dogs and blows into the gas chambers.

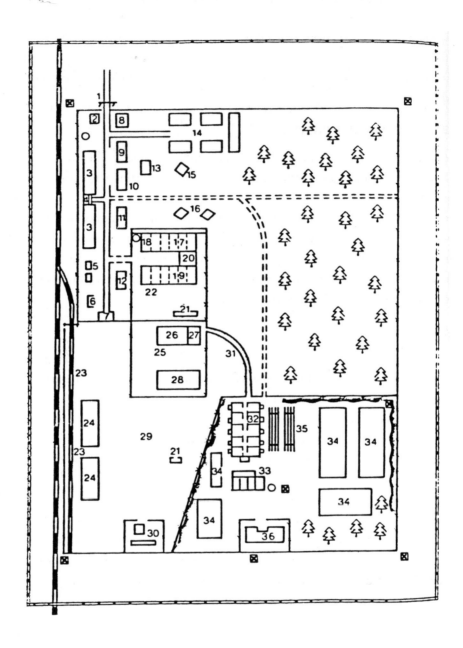

Figure 30. Treblinka camp, crematoria blocks 32 and 33

We know that others came from Poland:

> Once a transport of seventy Gypsies from near Warsaw was brought in. These men, women and children were destitute. All they had were some soiled underwear and ragged clothes . . . Within a few hours all was quiet and nothing left but their corpses.

In September 1944 another group of Gypsies was brought to Treblinka. They were told they could build a camp for themselves in the woods. The women lit fires and started to cook while the men were taken off to the woods. When the men reached the woods they found an open mass grave waiting for them. A hundred men were forced into the grave and shot. Some did not die at once. The rest were forced to cover them with earth, after which they too were pushed into the grave and shot. A thin layer of earth was used to cover their bodies.

When the women heard the machine-gun fire they realised that something was wrong and began to shout. The Nazis attacked the women with sticks and seized the small children, killing them by smashing their heads against the trees. The women and older children were then machine-gunned to death.

A group of Gypsies recaptured after trying to escape from the Warsaw ghetto was sent to Treblinka and killed, again with machine guns.

DEATH MARCHES

As the Soviet troops moved west the SS guards set about destroying the evidence of the concentration camps. Records were burnt, graves were dug up and the bodies burnt and the surviving prisoners were made to march day after day on foot towards Germany itself. One male Gypsy survived the death march from Auschwitz. As some sick inmates were left behind in many of the camps, including Auschwitz, it is hard to see the logic of these death marches. But then it is difficult to see the logic in much of Nazi policy.

In March 1945 a party of 242 Gypsy children who had come on foot from a number of camps arrived at Weddewarden camp. Here they only had two months' more imprisonment before they were freed by British and Canadian troops.

MEDICAL EXPERIMENTS

Gypsies interned in the concentration camps were regularly used as guinea pigs for experiments.[63] Dr Mengele at Auschwitz was only one among many who carried these out. Usually these led to death, maiming and disfigurement. Rarely was any regard paid to the pain and the suffering of the patients except by the prisoner nursing staff. Often the experiments were of doubtful or no scientific value and sometimes were simply another way of murdering unwanted human beings. The centres for the experiments were squalid and lacked medicines; circumstances mitigated heavily against recovery. Below the reader will find a short account of some of the experiments, representing only a fraction of those which took place. We have indicated where possible who was responsible for this hideous maltreatment of Gypsy prisoners.

Authority to use Gypsies seems to have rested ultimately with Himmler. For example, he gave agreement to serological experiments under Professor Werner Fischer on 9 June 1942. But SS General Oswald Pohl, from March 1942 Head of the Inspectorate of Concentration Camps, appears himself to have given permission for at least one set of experiments. No record exists to indicate that any difficulties were met in getting permission and it is obvious to us that authorisation was in fact freely given.

At one stage Himmler asked Ernst Grawitz, Chief Doctor of the SS, to obtain the opinions of Nebe and other Nazis on the use of prisoners for sea-water experiments. Grawitz replied, giving, among others, Nebe's ideas:

> I agree to the proposal to make an experiment to make sea-water drinkable. I suggest using the asocial Gypsy half-breeds in Auschwitz.

Grawitz said there were Gypsies healthy enough but not suitable for work, and that he was going to make a special suggestion to Himmler about it. He added:

> I think it right to choose the required number of guinea-pigs from these people. If Himmler agrees I will name the persons to be experimented upon.

In his communication to Himmler, Grawitz pointed out:

> Because the Gypsies are partly of a different racial composition they may produce results which cannot immediately be applied to our men. So it

is desirable that such prisoners who are similar to the European population should be made available for the experiments . . . I request your approval.

On behalf of Himmler, the Special Commissioner for Health Karl Brandt replied on 8 July 1944, saying he had agreed to Nebe's proposals.

At Natzweiler experiments with typhus took place. Both Gypsies and Jews, sent from Auschwitz and elsewhere, were infected with the disease. Those selected travelled for two weeks during mid winter locked in goods wagons. They had no heating and enough food only for four days so that many perished and others became seriously ill even before arriving at Natzweiler. Dr Chretien, a prisoner who worked in the camp hospital, relates how eighty Gypsies were used for these experiments early in 1944. Divided into two equal groups, they were separated and placed in two small, cramped rooms. Those in one room received vaccination against typhus while the others did not. Then the entire number was injected with typhus, returned to the rooms and locked in. Another report says six men including Gypsies were injected in the arm at the hospital. In consequence the whole length of the arm was scarred, pus erupted everywhere on the skin and the sores did not heal.

Salt water

Also in 1944 Gypsies came from Buchenwald, Sachsenhausen and elsewhere to a centre at Dachau for experiments involving injections with a solution of salt. It is claimed that some were volunteers. A witness reports that two volunteered only to get out of a punishment squad. Beigelböck, who was among those conducting the research, found some of the Gypsies had been drinking water and he flew into a rage, reproaching them with first volunteering and then disobeying the rules. A prisoner, Franz Blaha, an eyewitness to these experiments, says in his account that in the autumn of 1944 a group of some sixty Gypsies and Hungarians was locked up in a room for five days and given nothing except salt water. None died, probably because they received food smuggled in by other prisoners.

Mustard gas

Gypsies were used at Sachsenhausen for experiments with mustard gas. An anti-gas injection was also tested by Eickenbach at Natzweiler early in 1944. After injections, prisoners were put into a gas-filled room and four died.

When the experiment was repeated with a group of ten Gypsies in June, evidence shows that two who were not injected, as a control to the experiment, died. One of the survivors was then killed and dissected for an autopsy.

At Buchenwald twenty-six Gypsies received injections of spotted-fever virus on the orders of Pohl. Six of them died. At the same camp during 1942 four Gypsy women were used for experiments into the effect of freezing. Not everything is yet known about the activities of Dr Mengele who — it is believed — fled into hiding in South America after the war. It has been stated that he killed some Gypsies because their eyes were of a certain colour. He then sent the eyes to a Berlin institute. We also know that he used Gypsies in experiments at Auschwitz for injections with phenole and was particularly interested in twins and blood groups.

Anthropological tests

Some tests carried out on Gypsies were part of an attempt to prove their inferiority to Germans. With this aim, Himmler dispatched a selection of forty Gypsies to Sachsenhausen in spring 1942 for investigation by Professor Werner Fischer and Dr Hornbaek, both of whom had acquired experience while working on black prisoners of war and received permission to perform experiments on Gypsies. Hornbaek soon dropped out, however, because he was sent to the eastern front.

Sterilisation

One aspect of medical experimentation was particularly harrowing because of its long-term implications for Gypsies. This was the trials of sterilisation, one of the methods used in the attempt to destroy the Gypsy people. The Nazis wanted the labour of the living generation but were determined to prevent them from reproducing.

The Deputy Gauleiter for Lower Austria, Karl Gerland, wrote to Himmler on 24 August 1942, requesting that Dr Fehringer be permitted to conduct experiments with *Caladium* on the Gypsies in Lackenbach camp. This method of sterilisation, however, could not be adopted on a large scale because the climate in Germany was unsuitable for growing the plant.

During the Auschwitz trial, evidence was shown that Dr Lucas carried out sterilisation of men and women at Ravensbrück. A witness, Bruno Stein, said when he was in Auschwitz it was announced that ex-soldiers could

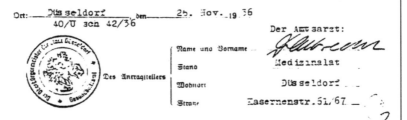

FIGURE 31. Document ordering the sterilisation of a Gypsy woman in 1936.

volunteer to be sterilised and would then be free. According to Stein, these ex-soldiers were put into a work party which built a platform, but they were not sterilised at that time. Later all were sent to Ravensbrück and sterilised there by Dr Lucas at the end of 1944. Stein himself was, in the event, not released but transferred to Sachsenhausen. Another witness stated that after the operation Gypsies were allowed to volunteer for military service. Some who did not were gassed.

Another witness was sterilised on 4 January 1945 and had to stay in the sick bay for a week afterwards. He recalls that at this time six persons were being sterilised daily. Another victim has recounted how he was sterilised without anaesthetic on 10 January. When he screamed Dr Lucas said, 'Be quiet, you swine!' He was in the hospital block for six weeks after the operation.

Dr Lucas himself claimed at his trial that he only operated three times for sterilisation. On other occasions the operations were a pretence and could be reversed. He claimed that Gypsies were so anxious to be sterilised in order to be released from the camp that he could not resist doing the operations. He was sentenced to three years in prison.

In 1945 Professor Carl Clauberg sterilised some 130 Gypsy girls who had been brought to Ravensbrück from Auschwitz. This was probably done by an injection into the uterus. The mothers of the girls signed forms of consent after being promised release. Several died and the survivors were not freed but transported to another camp. A twelve-year-old girl operated upon did not even have her abdominal wound sewn up after surgery, and died after several days of agony. In Auschwitz Dr Schumann had experimented with sterilising prisoners, including Gypsies, using X-rays.

Sterilisation also took place outside the camps, including that of 123 persons at Stettin. Gypsy women married to Germans were operated on at Dusseldorf-Lierenfeld. Julius Adler and his family from Schneidemuhl were sterilised. His wife died soon after the operation. Elfriede Dinschmidt was sterilised in an institution near Bielefeld in 1940 on the order of the Eugenics Court. The reason given: she was of mixed race. Lucia Strasdinsch, as a condition for being permitted to reside in Libau (Liepaja), in the USSR, had to undergo sterilisation on 9 January 1942, on the orders of Lieutenant Frank. There were many other Gypsies who survived the Nazi period but who could not bear children as a result, among them Tickno Gardner. Lined up to be gassed with other Gypsies, she escaped death by moving into another group of naked women nearby and was then put to work sorting clothes.

From the above information it is clear the practice was carried out in widely separated places and at different periods. In fact, sterilisation was one of the first measures suggested against Gypsies and the choice between this and internment had preoccupied some even in the pre-war Nazi period. Towards the end of the war, hospital facilities of every kind were needed for the increasing number of air-raid victims and this stopped sterilisation being practised on any large scale.

CONCLUSION

The question often asked is how many Gypsies — Roma and Sinti — died during the Nazi period? The answer is that we do not know. One difficulty is that not all Gypsies were registered as such in the camps, nor was every roadside killing recorded by the perpetrators. Adding up the figures we have given country by country would give a total of around 200,000 who were deliberately killed or died through starvation and lack of medical attention. It is likely that if full documentation were available this number would rise. If we add those who died in so-called euthanasia programmes, who were conscripted into the forces and labour brigades of the various combatants and who died at the front, and also those killed in air raids and bombardments, we may well be reaching the oft-cited figure of 500,000. It should be remembered, too, that the total number of deaths does not represent the full measure of the suffering of the Romanies and Sinti during the Nazi period. Of those not killed hundreds were interned in camps or prisons or suffered other restrictions on their liberty. Many had mental breakdowns as a result of this confinement, which was worse perhaps for nomadic Gypsies than for sedentary citizens. Others were engaged in forced labour on the land, in mines and factories.

Many survivors bore the marks of experiments carried out on them and others were unable to bear children after irreversible sterilisation operations. The birth rate dropped not only through direct interference but also through the separation of young men from their families, and the premature death of the elders meant that traditions were not passed on. The Nazi genocide left the Gypsy community scarred and after many years the wounds have not yet healed.

POSTSCRIPT:

THE TRIAL OF THE MAJOR WAR
CRIMINALS AT NUREMBERG (1945-6)

Although — as so many have commented — there were no Gypsy witnesses at the Nuremberg trial, the fate of the Roma and Sinti was not ignored. On 20 November 1945, at the opening of the trial, the indictment containing the accusations against the defendants was read out by Robert Jackson of the United States and Sir Hartley Shawcross for the United Kingdom. The killing of Gypsies alongside Jews was already mentioned at this stage.

It was said the accused Nazi leaders 'conducted a deliberate and systematic genocide in order to destroy particularly Jews, Poles and Gypsies and others'. This is only in reference to the occupied territories. There is no mention at this stage of the trial of the treatment of Gypsies within Germany itself.

In the section of the indictment dealing with concentration camps and medical experiments reference was made to the abuse of four female Gypsies at Dachau during experiments on the effect of extreme cold.

The eleven volumes of the trial proceedings themselves contain several references to Gypsies. The index to the English edition leads us to four references to 'gipsies' (*sic*), namely:

IV-56: Any Gypsies (as well as Jews, Russians and Ukrainians) in prison in Germany are to be handed over to the SS and sent to concentration camps.

VI-218: The liquidation of the Gypsy camp at Auschwitz August 1944 is dealt with briefly in two sentences (within the report of a survivor from the adjacent camp): 'There was one camp for Gypsies which towards August 1944 was completely gassed. The Gypsies came from all parts of

Europe including Germany.' The witness was a French inmate in the next camp, Mme Vaillant-Couturier.

VIII-313: Sterilisation of a woman in Libau (Latvia).

XI-373: 1,000 Jews and Gypsies executed by the Task Forces (*Einsatzgruppen*).

There were at least two more references to Gypsies during the trial, which are not indexed:

VI-244: Several hundred Gypsy children arrived at Buchenwald and were sent on to Auschwitz to be gassed (the evidence of a French prisoner).

I-264: A recaptured escapee in Mauthausen was executed to the music of a Gypsy band playing *J'attendrai* and *Bill Black Polka*.

The six references take up some seven sentences in the eleven volumes of the trial transcript. Of more importance for historians than the trial itself are the documents which were collected for the trial. They include much additional information relating to Gypsies and some have been consulted for this volume. The Wiener Library has most of them and they are indexed. The Imperial War Museum has a complete collection. In our earlier book, *The Destiny of Europe's Gypsies*, we (Grattan Puxon and I) cited seventy-five of the Nuremberg documents. These included German documents and the stories of survivors.

An important event for the accusations relating to Gypsies was the cross-examination of Kaltenbrunner on 11–13 April 1946 — the 105th–107th days of the trial. The defendant Kaltenbrunner was from 1943 head of the Central Security Headquarters (*RSHA*), which was responsible for concentration camps and the extermination programme for Jews. Kaltenbrunner accepted that all the killings had taken place in the camps and the occupied territories but denied any personal knowledge of them. He denied any knowledge of the reports of the Task Forces (*Einsatzgruppen*) and claimed that any of his signatures found on documents were made with rubber stamps or were later forgeries.

Kaltenbrunner was nevertheless found guilty and hanged on the night of 16/17 October 1946. Himmler — the prime policy-maker for Gypsies — had committed suicide well before the trial.

NOTES

Personal communications and correspondence are not cited in the notes, which have been kept to a minimum. The material Grattan Puxon and I have collected can be consulted in the Wiener Library in London. References have been included mainly to guide researchers to sources and occasionally where it was felt necessary to substantiate our account of events.

1. For an authoritative history of the Gypsies see A. Fraser, *The Gypsies* (Oxford, 1992).
2. W. Stuckart and H. Globke, *Kommentare zur deutschen Rassengesetzgebung*, Vol. 1 (Munich, 1936).
3. E. Justin, Lebensschicksale artfremderzogener Zigeunerkinder (Doctoral thesis, Berlin, 1944).
4. R. Ritter, 'Die Zigeunerfrage u. das Zigeunerbastardproblem', in *Fortschritte der Erbpathologie*, Pt. 1 (1939).
5. For Bader, see M. Zimmermann, *Rassenutopie und Genozid* (Hamburg, 1996), p. 410.
6. *Journal of the Gypsy Lore Society* (*JGLS*), series 3 xiii (1934), pp. 217–18.
7. R. Gilsenbach, 'Marzahn – Hitlers erstes Lager fur Fremdrassiger', *Pogrom*, 122 (1986), pp. 15–17.
8. Nuremberg Trial document NG-552; documents collected for the Nuremberg trial, Potsdam Zigeunerpolizeiakten (ZPA) 41.
9. ZPA 74.
10. See H.-J. Döring, 'Die Motive der Zigeunerdeportation vom Mai 1940', in *Vierteljahreshefte f. Zeitgeschichte*, Vol. 7 (October 1959), pp. 418–28; and H. Buchheim, 'Die Zigeunerdeportation vom Mai 1940', *Gutachten der IZG*, Vol. 1 (1958), pp. 51–9.
11. Eichmann Trial documents T 164 and 165. Eichmann was present at this meeting.

12. Nuremberg doc. NO-5322; Eichmann doc. T 166.
13. Allgemeine Heeres Mitteilung (Allg. H. Mitt., General Army Report) (1941), p. 82. See also ZPA 61.
14. Decree of the Ministry of Education 22.iii.1941.
15. National Archives (Alessandria, US) T 175 reel 461 frames 2980085–6.
16. Nuremberg doc. PS-654.
17. Nuremberg doc. L-179.
18. Himmler had evidently changed his mind since 20 April 1942, when he wrote in his appointment book: 'The Gypsies should not be exterminated.'
19. Report of the *Reichsicherheitshauptamt* (Central Security Headquarters) V A 2 2260/42. See also Zimmermann, *Rassenutopie und Genozid*, p. 481 n. 11.
20. Himmler files MA 3(9) in Institut f. Zeitgeschichte, Munich.
21. ZPA 46.
22. *RSHA* V A 40/43 11.i.43.
23. ZPA 62.
24. ZPA 49.
25. Nur. doc. NG-845.
26. Nur. doc. NG-684.
27. J. Knobloch, 'Volkskundliche Sinti-Texte', *Anthropos*, 45 (1950), p. 223–40. See also Document 611/5/8 in the Wiener Library.
28. S. Steinmetz, *Osterreichs Zigeuner im NS-Staat* (Vienna, 1966), p. 46.
29. C. Mayerhofer, *Dorfzigeuner* (Vienna, 1988), p. 47.
30. K. Ciechanowski, 'Das Schicksal der Zigeuner und Juden in den Jahren des zweiten Weltkrieges in Pommerellen'. Paper delivered at the Nazi War Crimes Conference in Warsaw, April 1983.
31. *Auschwitz-Hefte* (Auschwitz Museum, 1959). This publication contains a diary of events secretly kept by prisoners.
32. Reparations claims.
33. B. Richter, 'Auschwitz, matricola Z.1963', *Lacio Drom*, 2 (1965).
34. E. Bartels and G. Brun, *Gypsies in Denmark* (Copenhagen, 1943).
35. Evidence of Dr Beilin, session 69 of the Eichmann Trial.
36. *Die Zeit*, 9.v.46. Many other killings in Poland were reported at the Warsaw War Crimes Conference, 1983.
37. J. Ficowski, *Ciganie na polskich drogach* (Cracow, 1965), pp. 91–3.
38. *Welt der Arbeit*, 9.ix.1964, p. 8.
39. Ficowski, *Ciganie na polskich drogach*, p. 100.
40. Reparations claim LG (Landgericht) München I EK 705/51. State Court records.

41. J. Jovanović, 'La criminalité des Tsiganes: griefs et réalité', *Etudes Tsiganes*, 4 (1967), pp.12–15.

42. Nur. doc. NOKW-905.

43. Asylum claim. Dossier in the Wiener Library 611/8/1 (restricted access).

44. The records of the Task Forces (*Einsatzgruppen*) are taken from Trials of War Criminals (Green series) (TWC) vol. 4 and Nuremberg docs NO-2827 etc.

45. For this visit and the Task Forces in general, see R. Ogorreck, *Die Einsatzgruppen und die Genesis der Endlösung* (Berlin, 1996).

46. TWC vol. 4, pp. 286–7.

47. See P. Ariste, 'Estonian Gypsies', *JGLS*, xliii (1964), p. 60.

48. J. Kochanowski, 'Some notes on the Gypsies of Latvia', *JGLS*, xxv (1946), pp. 34–8 and 112–16.

49. H. Arendt, *Eichmann in Jerusalem* (New York, 1964), p. 188.

50. M. Bulajić, *Ustaški zločni genocida* (Belgrade, 1988). See also D. Asković, *Stradanja Roma u Jasenovcu* (Belgrade, 1994).

51. The scholar Rade Uhlik estimated at least 28,000: *JGLS*, series 3, xxvi (1947), p. 116.

52. B. Mezey (ed.) *A magyarországi cigánykérdés dokumentumokban* (Budapest, 1986).

53. As reported by the Jewish Black Book Committee (New York, 1946).

54. P. Radita, 'Tragedia degli Zingari rumani durante la guerra', *Lacio Drom*, 1(2) (1966), pp. 8–15.

55. Centre de Documentation Juive, Paris, Doc. CDXLIV-9.

56. See O. Nansen, *Fra dag til dag* (Oslo, 1946).

57. For Buchenwald, see E. Kogon, *Theory and Practice of Hell* (London, 1950).

58. *Auschwitz-Hefte*, Auschwitz Museum, 1959, is the source for much of the information in this section.

59. R. Höss, *Kommandant in Auschwitz* (Stuttgart, 1958).

60. See Zimmermann, *Rassenutopie und Genozid*, p. 340.

61. W. Gunther, *Ach, Schwester ich kann nicht mehr tanzen. Sinti und Roma im KZ Bergen-Belsen* (Hanover, 1990).

62. One survivor from Sobibor, Dov Freiburg, remembered the arrival there of a transport of Gypsies while an eyewitness, Maria Daniel, saw two truckloads of Gypsies passing through Rava Russkaya on the road to Belzec. The sources for Treblinka are: W. Grossman, *Die Hölle von Treblinka* (London, 1945); Y. Wiernik, *A year in Treblinka* (New York, 1945).

63. For the medical experiments in general, see A. Mitscherlich and F. Mielke, *Death Doctors* (London, 1962).

A CHRONOLOGY

1933   National Socialist Party takes power in Germany
Decree on the Prevention of Hereditarily Diseased Offspring
Dachau concentration camp built

1934   Expulsion of 'undesirable foreigners' from Germany

1935   Law for the Protection of German Blood and Honour
Citizenship Law
First internment camps for German Gypsies

1936   The Racial Hygiene and Population Biological Research Centre opened

1937   Decree on the Fight to prevent Crime

1938   Decree on the Fight against the Gypsy Menace
Gypsy Police Unit in Munich renamed National Centre for the Fight
against the Gypsy Menace and moved to Berlin
Germany invades Austria

1939   The Settlement Decree
Germany invades the Czech lands and Poland
Italy invades Albania
Second World War begins

1940   Deportations of Gypsies to Poland
Germany invades France, Belgium and Holland
Hungary and Romania join the Axis Treaty

1941   Classification of Gypsies into pure and 'half-breeds'
Gypsies not to be called up for military service
Germany invades Yugoslavia

1942   Lodz Gypsy ghetto liquidated
Wannsee Conference (Final Solution for Jews)
Croatian government orders the arrest of all Gypsies
Himmler issues the Auschwitz Decree

1943   German Gypsies sent to Auschwitz
Germany takes over north Italy

1944   Auschwitz Gypsy camp liquidated

1945   Soviet troops liberate Auschwitz
British troops liberate Bergen-Belsen
German army surrenders

FURTHER READING

The most authoritative work is the late Michael Zimmermann's *Rassenutopie und Genozid* (Hamburg, 1996), which contains, apart from the 509 pages of text and notes, an extensive bibliography. We also draw the attention of the reader to the three-part series published by the University of Hertfordshire Press entitled *The Gypsies during the Second World War* (Hatfield, 1997–2006). This gives greater coverage and more sources than was possible in this single volume for most of the countries in Nazi Europe, together with extensive references.

Books in English are few:

Rosenberg, O., *A Gypsy in Auschwitz* (London, 1999)

Sonnemann, T., *Shared sorrows* (Hatfield, 2002): describes the interaction of survivors of the Jewish and Romany genocide

Winter, W., *Winter time: memoirs of a German Sinto who survived Auschwitz* (Hatfield, 2004)

For individual countries:

Austria

Steinmetz, S., *Österreichs Zigeuner im NS-Staat* (Vienna, 1966)

Thurner, E., *National Socialism and Gypsies in Austria* (Tuscaloosa, Alabama, 1998)

Belgium

Gotovitch, J., 'Quelques données relatives à l'extermination des Tsiganes de Belgique', *Cahiers d'histoire de la Seconde Guerre Mondiale*, 4 (1976), pp. 161–80

Czechoslovakia

Nečas, C., *Československti Romové v Letech 1938–1945* (Brno, 1994)

——, *Holocaust českych Romu* (Prague, 1999)

France

Peschanski, D., Hubert, M.-C. and Philippon, E., *Les Tsiganes en France, 1939–1946* (Paris, 1994)

Holland

Sijes, J., *Vervolging van Zigeuners in Nederland 1940–1945* (S'Gravenhage, 1979)

Hungary

Barsony, J. and Daroczi, A., *Pharrajimos. The fate of the Roma during the Holocaust* (Budapest, 2007)

Norway

Hanisch, T., *Om Sigöynerspörsmålet* (Oslo, 1976)

Romania

Ioanid, R., *The Holocaust in Romania* (Chicago, 2000)

INDEX

The Gypsies during the Second World War

The University of Hertfordshire's seminal three-part
examination of the fate of Europe's Gypsies
at the hands of the Nazis

Volume 1 - From "Race Science" to the Camps
Karola Fings and Henriette Asséo, trans. D. Kenrick

This first volume focuses on Nazi anti-Gypsy
policies and their background, principles
and effects: internment, deportation and
extermination.

ISBN 978-0-900458-78-1
£12.75/$24.95

Volume 2 - In the Shadow of the Swastika
edited and translated by Donald Kenrick

This extensively illustrated second volume deals
with the persecution of the Romanis and Sinti in
some of the countries occupied by Germany and
its fascist allies.

ISBN 978-0-900458-85-9
£12.45/$24.95

Volume 3 - The Final Chapter
edited by Donald Kenrick

The concluding volume considers the fates of
those in countries not previously explored. It also
gives an overview of what happened after 1945,
and considers the future of the Roma in today's
Europe.

ISBN 978-1-902806-49-5
£14.99/$29.95

www.herts.ac.uk/UHPress
UHPress@herts.ac.uk

University of
Hertfordshire

University of Hertfordshire Press